FROM ASH TO WATER

FROM ASH TO WATER

Meditations on Lent

Luis Granados, DCJM

CLUNY *and* DIDASKALOS

Original Spanish edition:
De la ceniza al agua
(Madrid: Didaskalos, 2022)

American edition:
From Ash to Water
(Providence: Cluny and Didaskalos, 2025)

This American edition of *De la ceniza al agua* is published in the United States by Cluny Media LLC on behalf of Editorial Didaskalos.

NIHIL OBSTAT: Dr. Anthony Lilles, S.T.D., *Censor Librorum*

IMPRIMATUR: Samuel J. Aquila, *Archbishop of Denver*

For more information regarding Cluny and its work, please write to info@clunymedia.com, or to Cluny Media LLC, P.O. Box 1664, Providence, RI 1664
WWW.CLUNYMEDIA.COM

For more information regarding this title or the work of Editorial Didaskalos, please write to didaskaloseditorial@gmail.com, or to Calle Valdesquí 16, 28023, Madrid, Spain
WWW.EDITORIALDIDASKALOS.ORG

ISBN: 978-1685953973

Cover design by Clarke & Clarke
Cover image: Duccio di Buoninsegna, *Christ and the Samaritan Woman*, 1310–1311, tempera and gold on panel

CONTENTS

"LIFT UP YOUR STAFF and stretch out your hand over the sea, and split it in two, that the Israelites may pass through the sea on dry land" (Ex 14:16). In the passage of the Red Sea, the Lord drove back the sea with a strong wind. He opened a new path of life through the waters of death: forty years walking from the slavery of Egypt toward the Promised Land.

In this time of Lent, Jesus Christ invites us to start a path of forty days. He is the new Moses: through the gift of the Holy Spirit—a strong wind—he drives back the sea and offers us a path from the slavery of sin toward a new life. During this Lent we are invited, like the people of Israel, to glorify God and to walk through the waters of the Red Sea. These waters remind us of the gift of the new life we received the day of our Baptism. Christ grants us forty days to remember the gift of eternal life and to pray for those who will be baptized during the Easter Vigil.

Introduction

LUIS GRANADOS, DCJM

REMEMBER man that you are dust, you are ash, and to dust you shall return (see Gn 3:19). These words resound every Ash Wednesday, at the beginning of Lent. We hear them when ashes are placed in the form of a cross on our foreheads. This is our life; we are dust and to dust we shall return. Who will redeem us from this path toward death?

If this is the case, if we are like dust, perhaps the best response would be to follow the Latin poet Horace: "Seize the day" (*Carpe diem*). Let us live the present, without worries about the future. Do not ask too much. Just enjoy yourself. "While we are speaking, envious time will have already fled: seize the day, trusting as little as possible in the next day" (*Odes*, book 1, n. 11).

From ashes to water

The proposal of Jesus is very different from that of Horace. We are dust, ashes, but we are not called to live in a perpetual and insufferable search for pleasures while in this life. The same who said: Remember man that you are dust (see Gn 3:19), in the first pages of the Holy Scripture, proclaimed in the last page: "Behold, I make all things new" (Rev 21:5), even the dust and the ashes.

Lent is Jesus' proposal for you and me. In these forty days he wants to explain to us the path of our life. We are dust, we are like ashes, but through our encounter and friendship with him we become a new creature. If we remain in him we will receive the water of Easter and together with it, eternal life. From this point of view, these ashes are not just a sign of death, penance, and mortality. In them we can discover a sign of true hope. This way of hope is therefore the great path of Lent: from ash to water, from desert to paradise. We will begin Lent with Ash Wednesday and we will finish it with Easter, when we will receive the Water of Life.

Let me remind you that these ashes are not one of the seven sacraments instituted by Christ, but a sacramental, a sign instituted by the Holy Church. These ashes have been waiting for this moment more than ten months. They were made by burning palms blessed the previous Palm Sunday. They keep therefore a deep relationship with the Passion of Christ and with our prayer and praise: "Hosanna...; / blessed is he who comes in the name of the Lord" (Mt 21:9; Ps 118:26). If Jesus was able to give new life to Lazarus, and to transform stones into children of Abraham (see Jn 11; Mt 3:9), he will be able to transform us, our dust and ashes, into those palms which will be used to welcome Jesus as the King and Messiah.

From ashes to water. The path of Lent helps us to understand the path of our whole life. God has not created us as ashes. In the beginning God created us out of nothing through the love of our parents. The Bible says God formed us from the mud of the ground and blew into us his breath of life, his spirit: from nothing to mud and from mud to flesh. But then, the following page, we read about the lack of trust and the disobedience of Adam and Eve. Being friends of God, through sin they went from flesh to dust and ash. What's next? From ashes to nothing, to emptiness? Lent is the proclamation of good news. These ashes are called to receive the water that comes from the heart of Christ. What's next? A new creation: from ashes to a new life, to the life of the friends of God.

Meditations for Lent

Forty: time of trusting in God's power

As we can see, Lent is a special time in which we are called to trust in the power of God. These forty days recall the time of God's work on us. In the Holy Scripture, this number is highly symbolic and represents a long time in which God is purifying, transforming, and preparing us to encounter him. The main reference of these forty days is Jesus, who spent this time fasting in the desert before beginning his public ministry (see Mk 1:13; Lk 4:2).

But Jesus fasted "forty days and forty nights" in order to present himself as the fulfillment of the Old Testament. Of course we remember that Moses spent forty days on Mount Sinai when he was receiving the Law from God, and again another forty days a second time (see Ex 24:18; 34:28; Dt 9:9–25; 10:10). And later, due to their lack of faith, the Israelites will wander in the desert for forty years (see Ex 16:35; Nm 14:33–34). But we can consider many other examples. For example, the prophet Elijah traveled forty days to Mount Horeb to encounter God (see 1 Kgs 19:8); the prophet Jonah preached that Nineveh would be overthrown in forty days (see Jon 3:4); and the prophet Ezekiel lay on his right side for forty days to symbolize the sins of the people of Judah (see Ez 4:6). But even in the story of Noah and the Great Flood, it rained for forty days and forty nights (see Gn 7:4–17), and before David fought him, the Philistine Goliath taunted the Israelite army for forty days (see 1 Sm 17:16).

We could propose more examples, like the forty days of Jesus after his Resurrection and before ascending into heaven (see Acts 1:3). But what is important here is that "forty days" is a time in which God is working in the human heart. In the middle of the desert, God will open a path from the slavery of Egypt and the desert of Sinai, to the Promised Land, a new paradise. Through the preaching of the prophet Jonah, God will offer Nineveh forty days to convert and become a new city. Forty days is a long time in which God wants to show his power in our lives.

FROM ASH TO WATER

Memory of the future

Remember man that you are dust (see Gn 3:19). Remember. The work of God in these forty days begins with a call to exercise our memory. The Lord gives us these forty days to remember. What do we have to recall to our heart?

Remember man that your are dust…but the Lord has chosen you to be his disciple. Remember that the mercy and love of God endure for ever. Lent wants to remind you of the gift, of the great life you have received. Of course, this implies remembering the great moment in which the water of Easter changed your life: your baptism.

Lent is a special time to remember the great gift of becoming children of God in the Church. Baptism was the beginning of a new life in Christ. Later, you received the gift of your first confession, the embrace of the Father always open to the humble and meek. Then came your first communion, the Body of Christ, his company for your daily life, and your confirmation, the new strength and boldness of the Holy Spirit. You may continue, if it is the case, remembering the gift of marriage and parenthood, or the gift of priesthood and religious life.

Self-centered time? Not my path, but our path

If you want to remember your baptism, you cannot remain alone. Usually, you received your baptism as a child and you cannot remember anything unless you ask your parents, the priest, or your siblings. You were there, but unable to remember. Even if you were baptized as an adult, you need the others to remember better. To remember is a communitarian action. Isolated, I cannot remember well; isolated, I deform the past.

Lent is not my but our path, the path of my family toward Easter. It is not just time for myself, for my conversion, my spiritual growth… Sometimes we misunderstand Lent and we think of it in a self-centered way as a "narcissistic time." When we live Lent as an individualistic time, it becomes a really sad and hard time in which we are called to bow our head and repeat "I am nothing, I am nothing…"

But Lent is just the contrary. The heart of Lent is not myself but the others: those who need my alms, my prayer, and my fast. Lent is a time for my family, my community and for that reason, it is a time of joy. It is not the joy of Easter, of course, but the serene and deep joy of the pilgrim who walks with a great companion and friend. These forty days are not just for remembering that I am nothing, ash, a hopeless sinner…but to deepen the mystery of God's mercy. It is not about "I am nothing," but about "You, O God, are everything, and you called me to be with you." You need my "nothing," my poverty! For this reason, as Pope Francis reminded us, "the Church is not a refuge for the sad, but is the house of joy."

Lent is not self-centered time, but Christ-centered. We are invited to discover again the heart of Christ and enter the mystery of his life. We are invited to become a disciple of his heart. When we look at Christ, we are called to participate in his great love. For that reason, as a Christ-centered time, Lent is calling us to give alms, pray, and fast for those in need. Lent is calling us to forget about ourselves, our sufferings, struggles, worries…and take care of the suffering of the others. How are my spouse, my children, my parents, my siblings and friends, my neighbors…doing? I invite you to read these short meditations each day together with your family, perhaps right after dinner. And as a Christ-centered time, Lent is a special time of mission. Go out and announce the Gospel of the Lord!

Prepare the joy, prepare the feast

Therefore, we can understand now that Lent is not a time for sadness but for hope. The joy of Easter will be possible if we prepare it in this time of Lent. As a feast or the celebration of a party, the joy needs to be prepared. To receive the everlasting joy of Christ, we need to walk with him toward Jerusalem. We need to participate, to share in his joys and sufferings, and this will imply sacrifice, penance, fasting, alms-giving…

Let us begin this path. Lent is a privileged time of interior pilgrimage toward him who is the fount of mercy. It is a pilgrimage in which Christ himself accompanies us through the desert of our poverty, sustaining us on our way toward the intense joy of Easter (Benedict XVI, Message for Lent, 2006).

It is our path, the path of our family, perhaps reading together these pages every evening after dinner. Let us go with Jesus toward Jerusalem. "Let us also go to die with him" (Jn 11:16). We are those who suffer with the Lamb and will be blessed and reign with him for ever.

Time for great choices

Begin this Lent with great desires in your heart. Lent is a very special time for great choices. Perhaps you are high schooler, junior or senior, or you are already in college and you want to know the project of God for your life. You desire to be saint and friend of Christ and you want to know if the Lord is calling you to a special vocation, to a consecrated life. Or perhaps you are already on the path of holiness of marriage and family, or priesthood and religious life. In any case, this Lent is a time for conversion and for remembering how generous is the Lord with you. Ask the Lord: "What do you want me to do?"

I invite you to begin this Lent with the heart of Paul and Zacchaeus. Like Paul, be radical, available to change your projects and desires, your college, the schedule and agenda of your family, the way you speak about your spouse…if Jesus asks you to do so. Like Zacchaeus, be generous and offer your house, your talents, your whole life to the Lord. He is the great treasure. Do not be afraid. Do not set any limit to his action!

Meditations for Lent

From ash to water: Look at Christ, encounter him, follow him

Lent is a Christ-centered time. Jesus will be the focus of these forty days. We will look at him, encounter him, and finally follow him. In the first two weeks of Lent, we will look at him in order to know his heart. In the following three weeks we will encounter the mystery of Christ, who is calling us to love him more and more. And finally, as a consequence of this knowledge and love, we will hear his voice: Follow me!

As poor and dirty ashes, we need first of all for Jesus to look at us. His compassionate gaze is the beginning of our hope. His eyes, like the rays of the sun, have a special power. When Jesus looks at us, we can answer with our eyes and look at him.

For the first two Sundays of Lent, on two different mountains we will see Jesus suffering the temptations of the devil and revealing his glory in the Transfiguration. We will look at one of us, our brother, who is the Son of God, the Light of the World.

After looking at Christ and knowing him better, we are called to encounter him and enter into a new life. During the next three Sundays we will consider the life of three persons who met Christ and discovered a new horizon in their path. The Samaritan woman, the blind man, and the dead Lazarus encountered Jesus and discovered the Source of Life, the Light of the World, and the Eternal Life. Looking at Christ as Water, Fire, and Resurrection, we will remember the gift of our baptism.

The two last weeks of Lent are an invitation to follow Christ. Have you ever thought, where was the Samaritan woman during the Passion of Jesus? And the courageous blind man and the best friend Lazarus? We don't know where they were during those days. We will know it in heaven, when we will be able to speak with them and ask lots of things about Jesus. We can guess in any case, as it happened with John and Peter—and even with Judas—that they were not indifferent to the sufferings of Christ. They followed him with their weakness and fear and they suffered with his sufferings.

I

Looking at Christ

"AT the sight of the crowds, his heart was moved with pity" (Mt 9:36). The Gospels show us how Jesus was looking at the people with great love, as the shepherd looks at his flock. This compassionate "gaze" of Christ continues to fall upon individuals and peoples today, also upon us (Benedict XVI, Message for Lent 2006). Jesus is the shepherd who chooses to defend his flock from the wolves even at the cost of his own life.

During this time of Lent we want to look at Christ and at ourselves, at our ash. But in order to do that, we need first to discover his compassionate gaze on us. In the first days of Lent we will begin considering we are dust, ash, but this ash will be transformed by the merciful eyes of Jesus into a new creature. If we move forward we will discover the mystery of Jesus. He can look at us with such compassion because at the same time he is the Son of God. He is always under the tender eyes of the Father who sees what is hidden!

Under these eyes, we can now look at ourselves and at the others. Our gaze upon ourselves and upon mankind has to be measured against that of Christ. Fasting and almsgiving, together with prayer, are suitable means for us to become conformed to this "gaze."

We will see Christ on the mount of the Temptations, one with us. He knows our struggles. He has walked in trust and obedience to the Father. He is our friend. In the mystery of the Transfiguration we will see the fruit of the work of the Holy Spirit. After these thirty-three years of life, his face and flesh reveal the glory of God.

In the desert and the temptations we discover our Master and companion. Now, in the beauty and joy of Mount Tabor, we see our hope. In the middle of sufferings, we see the face of Christ, shining in splendor.

OUR ASH: OUR PILGRIMAGE

(ASH WEDNESDAY TO THE FIRST SUNDAY OF LENT)

Ash Wednesday

GOSPEL: MT 6:1–6,16–18

Jesus said to his disciples: "Take care not to perform righteous deeds in order that people may see them; otherwise, you will have no recompense from your heavenly Father. When you give alms, do not blow a trumpet before you, as the hypocrites do in the synagogues and in the streets to win the praise of others. Amen, I say to you, they have received their reward. But when you give alms, do not let your left hand know what your right is doing, so that your almsgiving may be secret. And your Father who sees in secret will repay you.

"When you pray, do not be like the hypocrites, who love to stand and pray in the synagogues and on street corners so that others may see them. Amen, I say to you, they have received their reward. But when you pray, go to your inner room, close the door, and pray to your Father in secret. And your Father who sees in secret will repay you.

"When you fast, do not look gloomy like the hypocrites. They neglect their appearance, so that they may appear to others to be fasting. Amen, I say to you, they have received their reward. But when you fast, anoint your head and wash your face, so that you may not appear to be fasting, except to your Father who is hidden. And your Father who sees what is hidden will repay you."

(1) *Our ash and our desire for God*

After the forest was burnt, nothing remained. Just ashes and smoke, some black and dead trees, witness of the beautiful pine trees devoured by the flames. Ashes. Ashes are the lack of water and water is a synonym of life. Around sixty to seventy percent of our organism is water. Some animals, like the jellyfish, are about ninety-five percent water. Ashes are precisely the lack of life, what remains of a living creature after the fire.

We don't begin this Lent with self-contentment but with ashes on our foreheads. The beginning of Lent, the beginning of wisdom is to recognize who I am: ashes which need water. I need help, I need a Savior. On the first day of Lent, tell Jesus: I need you! In order to be happy, to fulfill my vocation, and follow my mission as son or daughter, student, friend, husband or wife, father or mother, grandfather or grandmother... I need your presence, O Lord!

We need the Lord. Think about the ashes in the fireplace right after the flame is gone. If you pour water over them, they will "drink" the water because they are still very hot, they are "thirsty." Likewise, we need water, we need the presence of the Lord in our life. At the beginning of this Lent renew your thirst for the Lord. "O God, you are my God— / it is you I seek! / For you my body yearns; / for you my soul thirsts, / In a land parched, lifeless, / and without water" (Ps 63:2).

Ash means death. The liturgy reminds us today that we are not just mud or flesh, but dust, ash, because of our sin. There is no water in us; we need the life of Christ, our reconciliation with him.

(2) *Your Father sees what is hidden*

In today's Gospel, Jesus helps us to understand who we are. We are ashes and we need the presence of the Lord. Several times Jesus will speak about our Father who sees what is hidden. We need repetition. When we were kids, our mother used to ask us: Have you prayed today? Have you cleaned your room? Have you done your homework? Sometimes she had to repeat the same question one, two, or three times so that we remember and do it. Likewise, Jesus with us. He repeats insistently: Remember the presence of your Father who sees what is hidden.

This reminder is the mystery of our ashes; our Father sees what is hidden. We live under his merciful eyes, and this gaze fills us with hope. We are like ashes, but God is looking at us and—with his eyes—he will transform us (see Mt 6:18). When the Father looks at us and sees ashes, he also discovers our future, a promise full of hope: a sinner called to be forgiven and become a saint, a great friend of Christ.

Our Father sees what is hidden. What is he seeing? Alms, prayer, and fasting are three activities for this Lent. We are called to give alms, pray, and fast, but to do this in secret so that our Father who sees in secret will repay us. If we give alms, or pray, or fast blowing a trumpet before us or standing in the street corners so that others may see us, then we will have no reward. We are called to do these things before our Father, who sees the heart, what is invisible.

Therefore, the secret for this Lent is not just giving alms, fasting, and praying. The true treasure of this time is God, our Father. We are called to discover his presence in our lives. Alms, fast, and prayer will help us to understand the Father is our true possession and richness, our true food and our Beloved.

Let us consider it again. We are like ash. We are not nothing and we are not just evil, negative existence. We are ashes. If used with caution, wood ashes can be used as a fertilizer of our garden. Ashes contain most of the essential nutrients several plants need to thrive. For this reason, ashes are not just a sign of death but also a promise of new life. When God looks at our forehead marked with ashes, he sees children of God walking toward him. We are ashes, we are sinners, but we are not just evil. God looks at us and rejoices in our existence.

(3) *Be reconciled to God*

Under the eyes of God, we can be trustful. There is a powerful energy in the eyes of a father. When his father is looking at him, the child plays better during the football game, he studies better... Our parents' gaze gives us trust and peace: they are looking at us, they are taking care of us.

At the beginning of Lent we remember God our Father is looking at us and is calling us to be reconciled to him. "Yes. I will go to my Father." Lent is a wonderful time for a sincere and complete confession of your sins. "Yes, go to your Father."

Finally, as we heard in today's reading, we don't want to come alone to the Father, to confession. Become "ambassadors for Christ" (see 2 Cor 5:20–6:2). When you come to your frequent (monthly) confession, do not come alone. Bring a friend to the Lord!

For your prayer: Act of Presence of God

The very beginning of prayer is, like Jesus says, to recognize the presence of God the Father, who sees what is hidden, who sees in secret. This fact is not called to cause fear and anxiety in us, but just the opposite, peace and serenity. Nothing is hidden to our Father and for that reason we can be full of joy; he, our Father, knows everything.

At the beginning of your prayer consider who is before you, who is with you, who is going to hear you and speak to you. Be filled of reverence, awe, and gratitude.

Repeat: *O Lord, I know you are here with me. Thank you for your presence, thank you for being here. I believe in you, I adore you, I hope in you, I love you. I ask you for those who do not believe in you, do not adore you, do not hope in you, and do not love you. Help me to believe in you more every day, to adore you better, to hope in you and to love you always more.*

Thursday after Ash Wednesday

GOSPEL: LK 9:22–25

Jesus said to his disciples: "The Son of Man must suffer greatly and be rejected by the elders, the chief priests, and the scribes, and be killed and on the third day be raised."

Then he said to all, "If anyone wishes to come after me, he must deny himself and take up his cross daily and follow me. For whoever wishes to save his life will lose it, but whoever loses his life for my sake will save it. What profit is there for one to gain the whole world yet lose or forfeit himself?"

(1) *A great path of small steps*

Let us begin this path. We are like ash, but the Lord needs that we follow him. To follow him implies to take up our cross daily and follow him (see Lk 9:22–25). We begin Lent with this word of consolation and hope: Follow me! We are not supposed to walk alone during Lent. Jesus is opening the path. He walks with us, he walks before us. He will be with us.

But we are called to follow Jesus taking up our cross. Christ is not offering a romantic and easy path. To follow him implies effort, getting tired, and perseverance. Great things imply great efforts. If you want to climb a fourteener, you will need to overcome many difficulties. If you want to go ahead with these studies or that business...if you want to remain faithful in your marriage...you know it will not be easy at all. "The Son of Man must suffer greatly" (Lk 9:22). The greatest work ever performed, the work of our redemption, includes great suffering and sacrifice. And here comes the great news of Lent: you can offer your sufferings and difficulties with his.

A popular Christmas carol speaks about the good King Wenceslaus, who barefoot, was giving alms to the poor. His page was following him and was complaining about the snow and the cold weather. Then Saint Wenceslaus asked the servant to follow him through the deep snow: Put your feet, step by step, in my footprints! The servant began to do that and from that moment his feet were warmed up. To follow Jesus is something similar. We follow him and it is not just my cross, but ours. From that moment on, this yoke is completely different. Whoever believes is never alone, but always following him.

(2) *Gaining the whole world but losing himself?*

He heard this call but he was reluctant. He had just finished high school and was beginning college at the University of Paris. He was a good Catholic: coming to Sunday Mass and with daily prayers and frequent confession. Perhaps he was even helping with catechesis to kids of the parish... What profit is there for one to gain the whole world yet lose himself? These words were resounding in his heart at every moment. He was restless. His friend, Ignatius of Loyola, a little bit older than him, was always repeating these words of Jesus: Francis, what profit is there for you to gain the whole world, yet...?

But there were other friends, also Christians but more "normal" and funnier than Ignatius, more "light." There was a nice professor and students, offering him a life of parties, pleasure, money, and good business...

Francis Xavier was a good Christian and a very gifted and athletic student. In his heart there was a great battle between his vocation to holiness—the words of Jesus pronounced by Ignatius—and his lowest and smallest desires of a comfortable and easy life. He was trying to avoid the call of the Lord by offering to the Lord, not everything, but just a part of his heart. I will serve you, Lord, but here, in this job and place. I will work for you, but let me choose the time, the place, and the way.

> See, I have today set before you life and good, death and evil. If you obey the commandments of the LORD...you will live.... If, however, your heart turns away and you do not obey...I tell you today that you will certainly perish.... Choose life, then, that you and your descendants may live. (Dt 30:15–20)

Choose life: offer yourself to the Father with Christ.

What profit is there for one to gain the whole world...yet lose himself? Again this powerful word was coming to his heart. Nonsense. If I am to follow Jesus, then how can I remain lukewarm? I will offer myself without limits, without mediocrity. After a long prayer retreat with Ignatius, Francis Xavier answered with great generosity to the Lord. He gave a radical yes. Wherever you send me, whenever and whatever you ask me to do... I will do it.

(3) *Take up your cross daily*

Jesus asks us to follow him every day. We may think of the great heroism of St. Francis Xavier, traveling from Portugal to India, the Maluku Islands, Japan, and almost China... We may think of his hands, almost unable to continue baptizing so many hundreds of Indians daily, and his courageous adventures, risking his life at every moment. I will do the same. Nice desires the Lord may plant in your heart. The same thing happened to Saint Ignatius when he was reading the lives of the saints: Saint Francis of Assisi did this… I also have to do it!

Great desires. That sounds good but it can be very "romantic." These great desires will become actions through small steps. Saint Francis Xavier arrived in Japan with no connecting flights, but after spending months of his life on a ship, sailing all around Africa, and almost dying on several occasions through this great adventure. But everything began in Xavier, the small castle where his mother taught him the catechism and prayed with him. Everything began in Paris, where he encountered Christ through the words of Saint Ignatius of Loyola. And everything continued in Bologna, a beautiful Italian town where he spent many months taking care of the sick in a hospital. The people would see him praying, working, resting, speaking… and would say: Here is a man of great desires.

Great desires and great actions. But all this came through the small actions and steps in Spain, France, Italy, Portugal and then in the mission. Saint Francis Xavier was saving the world when he was obeying his mother in the castle of Xavier, when he was cleaning a room of the hospital in Italy, when he was healing the wounds of a poor leper, when he was praying to the Father, who sees in secret.

Let us learn well this point: if you want to follow Christ, if you want to be a hero, a great saint, choose the path of the small steps, the baby steps. Study this page of this book, offer this sacrifice for this person, pray this rosary, be faithful to this daily prayer today. Small steps will guide you toward great desires and actions.

For your prayer: Gratitude.

After the act of the presence of God, as his continuation, I invite you to give thanks to the Lord. Today give thanks because he is calling you to great things.

Thank you for calling me to love, to be holy. You want me to become a saint, a hero, a wise person in my daily life. You want me to take care of my relationships: in my family, my studies, my job. Thank you for trusting me, for giving me this great responsibility.

Friday after Ash Wednesday

GOSPEL: MT 9:14–15

Then the disciples of John approached him and said, "Why do we and the Pharisees fast much, but your disciples do not fast?" Jesus answered them, "Can the wedding guests mourn as long as the bridegroom is with them? The days will come when the bridegroom is taken away from them, and then they will fast."

(1) *Why are you fasting?*

Jesus fasted for forty days in the desert right before the temptations. After that long sacrifice, we know he began to eat and attend banquets in different places, in the houses of the disciples, the Pharisees, the tax collectors...

In today's Gospel, Jesus helps us to understand the sense of fasting. The disciples of John come to ask him: Why do we fast much but your disciples do not fast? (see Mt 9:14). The absence of fast is for them a sign of something strange and different.

As he does so many times, Jesus answers with another question: "Can the wedding guests mourn as long as the bridegroom is with them?" (Mt 9:15). To fast is to mourn, to manifest I am not ok, but I need the coming of someone to my life. You fast, Jesus says, because you await the coming of the Messiah. But here I am. Do not wait any more. Do not fast now. I am with you. But then Jesus continues: "The days will come when the bridegroom is taken away from them, and they will fast" (Mt 9:15). These days have arrived. We are those who are called to fast.

Why do we fast then? Fasting is not just about "not eating." Sometimes we don't eat because we are preparing for some tests before surgery or because we want to lose weight... But this is not the fast of Lent. Fasting is an act of love, a witness of our great desire for the presence of Jesus. We are waiting for his coming. So we fast.

We need to fast because we need to grow in this desire, this hunger, of his coming. Our friend and Lord —the Bridegroom—is coming! Fasting, we understand that only one thing is really necessary: the presence of Jesus in our life. We fast because we want to remember and increase our hunger for God.

Let us fast then. Let us fast, but not just of food. Fast of your self, of thinking about you, of wasting time with the internet... Can you fast there? How much time could you then devote to your family, your studies, your prayer, your good readings?

Let us fast, but always out of love. In a Russian monastery there was an old spiritual father known for his sacrifices and fasting. Once they found him eating a generous dinner with one of the brothers of the community. This brother had arrived sad and burdened from a long trip. And this spiritual father told him: "Let us eat together. Love is more important than fasting."

(2) *Miserere*

As you remember, when we fast, we are called to fast before our Father who sees in secret. Fasting helps us to recognize our poverty. When we experience hunger and thirst we understand we are very poor and fragile, we are needy.

Pope Francis helps us to understand the atmosphere of our fast. In one of his first interviews he was asked: Who is the Pope? He answered with simplicity: A sinner. No surprise. The pope is a sinner. It is not false humility but the pure truth. But the great announcement comes with the second word of Pope Francis. I am a sinner, but one who has been forgiven by the Lord: a sinner forgiven.

Today, when you fast, pray with Psalm 51 which is called the Miserere according to its first word: Have mercy (Miserere). In the Psalm we ask for a "contrite heart," that is, a humble heart which is not excusing himself and accusing the others. The heart of Adam accused Eve: "The woman whom you put here with me—she gave me fruit from the tree, so I ate it" (Gn 3:12). The heart of David was a contrite heart. After his great sin of adultery and murder, Nathan the prophet came to him, told him a story and accused him: "That man is you!" Then David, inspired by the Spirit, wrote Psalm 51: "Have mercy on me, God, in accord with your merciful love; / in your abundant compassion blot out my transgressions" (Ps 51:3).

Don't try to excuse yourself. Don't accuse others. Very good things begin with: I am sorry. Forgive me. Acknowledge the truth of your life: I am a sinner. I need help.

(3) *The courage of forgiveness*

Psalm 51 is a strange Psalm. It begins with the fear and humility of a great sinner, asking for mercy and compassion, and it ends with the boldness and courage of a missionary, called to teach transgressors the ways of the Lord. During this prayer, a transformation happens in the heart of David.

David looks at his sins and is tempted to despair. "For I know my transgressions; / my sin is always before me / … I have done what is evil in your eyes" (Ps 51:5–6). But the beginning of his prayer will save him. He has centered his attention on the action of God: "Have mercy on me, God / … In your abundant compassion blot out my transgressions" (Ps 51:3). I may be a sinner, but your actions are always greater. Based on this confidence, David begins to change the tone of his speech. "Cleanse me with hyssop, that I may be pure; / wash me, and I shall be whiter than snow" (Ps 51:9). This hope in God's compassion even moves him to rejoice: "You will let me hear gladness and joy…" (Ps 51:10).

We find the climax of the Psalm in the wonderful petition of David: "A clean heart create for me, God; / renew within me a steadfast spirit" (Ps 51:12). From now on, joy fills the heart of King David. He receives the joy of God's help, he teaches transgressors the ways of the Lord, his mouth declares the praise of God... This boldness comes from David's trust in God's infinite mercy. "Though your sins be like scarlet, / they may become white as snow; / Though they be red like crimson, / they may become white as wool" (Is 1:18).

Be reconciled to God! Like David before Nathan, this weekend can be a wonderful occasion to come to confession. With humility, with no excuses. You are before the Lord, your Maker and Father. Do not be afraid.

Yesterday we considered the great desires and actions of St. Francis Xavier. We only understand the achievements of this heroic missionary if we consider his trust in the Lord. The greatness of our desires and actions is only possible because of the greatness of God's compassion!

For your prayer: Pray with humility

After your act of presence of God and your moment of gratitude, pray with Psalm 51, the Miserere. You can ask the Lord the gift of a contrite and humble heart. O Lord, you know me, you know everything about me. Help me to understand that I need you, that without you I can nothing.

Saturday after Ash Wednesday

GOSPEL: LK 5:27–32

Jesus saw a tax collector named Levi sitting at the customs post. He said to him, "Follow me." And leaving everything behind, he got up and followed him. Then Levi gave a great banquet for him in his house, and a large crowd of tax collectors and others were at table with them. The Pharisees and their scribes complained to his disciples, saying, "Why do you eat and drink with tax collectors and sinners?" Jesus said to them in reply, "Those who are healthy do not need a physician, but the sick do. I have not come to call the righteous to repentance but sinners."

(1) *Eating with sinners*

Yesterday we saw Jesus speaking about fasting. The Pharisees and the disciples of John were fasting much, but the disciples of Jesus were not fasting because they were the wedding guests, the friends of Christ, the Bridegroom. Today Jesus confirms these words, eating and drinking with a large crowd of tax collectors.

Levi, a new disciple of his heart, gives a great banquet for Jesus in his house. And again the question of the Pharisees and scribes is aroused: Why do you eat? Why don't you fast? But now the scandal is greater, the matter is even worse: not only does he eat, but he eats... with tax collectors and sinners!

We know very well the meaning of eating with someone. It is not just a matter of enjoying the dialogue with the other. When we eat with the other, we manifest our desire of building a communion, a covenant with this person. In the case of Jesus and Matthew, the desire is stronger, because they are not just eating in a nice restaurant: Jesus comes to Matthew's house. Jesus accepts to bless this dwelling with his presence.

Jesus eats with sinners. If you want to share a meal with him, first of all, you need to acknowledge your truth: I am sick, I am a sinner. I need to be forgiven, I need to be reconciled to God. I need you, Jesus, I need the physician!

This is the beginning of wisdom, the beginning of greatness: acknowledge your meanness, your lack of power, your nothing.

(2) *Follow me*

Matthew's vocational call is very short and effective. Two words of Jesus are enough: Follow me! Matthew has good ears and answers with a radical action. Leaving everything behind, he gets up and follows him. Look at the example of the sinner, the tax collector. Others, like Peter and John, like Philip, need more time and explanations. Others, like the young rich man, a "good Catholic," resist the call of the heart of Jesus, and prefer his comfortable life and his bank accounts to Jesus. Matthew, the public sinner, answers quickly and without fear.

And then hear the words of Jesus: Follow me! Jesus is offering Matthew a great path. Think about Levi or Matthew. If he stays there as a tax collector, ignoring the two words of Jesus, he will remain as Levi, the sinner, one more among the tax collectors of Galilee. If he leaves everything behind he will become Matthew, the great apostle, one of the twelve, and one of the four evangelists. Jesus needs him and calls him. We do not find Matthew any more sitting at the customs post, but preaching and writing, docile to the inspiration of the Holy Spirit. His testimony and writing reach the ends of the earth in space and time.

Look at Matthew and don't think any more that you are just called "not to sin," just to be healed from your illness. You are called to help the physician. It happens like in those hospitals in times of war or in places in which there is a lack of personnel. As soon as one is healed from his wounds, he is called to help the surgeon or the physician, who is healing others. Don't think your life is just called to avoid sin, to take away what is evil... You are called to be fruitful, to grow in what is beautiful, good, and true. In every Christian we can discover a missionary, an apostle.

If you don't believe me, look at Matthew. As soon as he became a disciple, he gave a great banquet for Jesus and invited a large crowd of tax collectors. He wanted them to know and follow Jesus, together with him. Like Saint Bernard, who entered religious life with a large number of friends and relatives, Matthew wanted to share with his friends, public sinners like him, the joy of encountering Jesus. As soon as you become a disciple, you are called to become an apostle, a missionary. Go and give what you have received: the forgiveness of your sins, the beauty of the Sunday Mass…

(3) *Mary, the disciple of the heart of Jesus*

Mary was following Jesus during his public life. We don't know about the relationship between Mary and the apostles. We can imagine Mary would be close to those who where the closest friends and disciples of her Son. She wanted to know them and help them in their friendship with Christ.

We can think that between Mary and Matthew there was a good connection. In her immaculate heart, she understood very well the mystery of Matthew. A great sinner was called to proclaim the greatness of the Lord. We may imagine Mary helped Matthew to proclaim the greatness of the Lord, to rejoice in God his Savior, because he had looked with favor on his lowly servant.

For your prayer: Mary is with us in this pilgrimage.

You can begin your prayer as always, remembering the presence of Jesus with you (act of presence of God) and with a moment of gratitude. Then I invite you to pray the Magnificat, like Matthew with Mary. My soul proclaims the greatness of the Lord. Imagine you repeat the same words of Mary and you apply them to your life. Does this make sense? The Almighty has done great things for me… Now pray the Magnificat for the future of your life: My soul will proclaim the greatness of the Lord…for he will look with favor on his lowly servant…

It would be great if you learn the Magnificat by heart and you keep it in your memory, in your heart, in your mouth. Instead of complaining or gossiping, let us glorify our Lord, let us proclaim his greatness.

THE TEMPTATIONS: OUR COMPANION OFFERS US A NEW HEART

(FIRST WEEK OF LENT)

After the first four days of Lent, today we begin the first week of Lent. We will look at Christ, tempted on the mountain, and we will discover him as our companion—one of us—and as our Master, who offers us a new heart, a new mind.

First Sunday of Lent (A)

GOSPEL: MT 4:1–11

At that time Jesus was led by the Spirit into the desert to be tempted by the devil. He fasted for forty days and forty nights, and afterwards he was hungry. The tempter approached and said to him, "If you are the Son of God, command that these stones become loaves of bread." He said in reply, "It is written: / One does not live on bread alone, / but by every word that comes forth / from the mouth of God." Then the devil took him to the holy city, and made him stand on the parapet of the temple, and said to him, "If you are the Son of God, throw yourself down. For it is written: / He will command his angels concerning you / and with their hands they will support you, / lest you dash your foot against a stone." Jesus answered him, "Again it is written, / You shall not put the Lord, your God, to the test." Then the devil took him up to a very high mountain, and showed him all the kingdoms of the world in their magnificence, and he said to him, "All these I shall give to you, if you will prostrate yourself and worship me." At this, Jesus said to him, "Get away, Satan! It is written: / The Lord, your God, shall you worship / and him alone shall you serve." Then the devil left him and, behold, angels came and ministered to him.

(1) *The sign of his great love for us*

Right after receiving the Holy Spirit in the baptism, the Spirit guides Jesus to the desert, in order to be tempted by the devil (see Mt 4:1). Like all of us, Jesus is tempted. The mystery we consider today is not just something that happens, but something chosen by Christ; he wants to go to the desert and be with us in our temptations and doubts.

But this experience is not the only moment in which he will be tempted. Right before his Passion, in the Garden of Gethsemane, the devil will come again. And Jesus will also be tempted in many ways during his three years of preaching. The Temptations are a kind of anticipation, a condensed summing up of the life of Jesus. In them, Christ reveals to us his great love and his victory over sin.

Jesus is one of us, someone who has suffered with us: our companion. He wants to enter the drama of human existence in order to save us, the lost sheep. He has become like us, his brothers, and he has been tested in every way, yet without sin (see Heb 2:17; 4:15). For this reason he is able to sympathize with our weakness.

(2) *Metanoia: a new way of living, a new humanity, a new heart*

But we can go further in this mystery. Jesus is tempted, not only to sympathize with us, but also to help us overcome our temptations. He wants to offer us a new heart, a new mind. The time of temptation can be a time of growth and conversion, in which we rediscover what is really important in our life. The temptation is not a sin, but an occasion of growth, of understanding that without him, we can do nothing. Remember the saying of a great monk, Saint Anthony, Abbot: "Whoever is not tempted, he will not be saved."

In any case, when we experience temptation we should not say "I am being tempted by God," but rather "God wants to be with me and help me to overcome this temptation" (see Jas 1:13). The devil—not God—is the tempter and the liar.

In the temptations of Jesus, we will see the devil using and quoting the Holy Scripture. Don't be surprised. As Vladimir Soloviev proposed in his Anti-Christ, the devil knows the bible very well. In his tale, Soloviev presents the devil as "doctor honoris causa" from the Tubinga University. The devil knows the word of God and tries to use it against God. He reads and uses the bible against its Author, our Lord. If we want to read and understand the Holy Scripture, we cannot do it alone; we need the help and guidance of our mother, the Church.

The devil using the Holy Scripture! When we see this, we can understand the power of temptation. Every temptation has an important element of truth and goodness. For this reason it is attractive to us. The closer the temptation is to the truth, the more dangerous it is. Imagine you are a wife and mother of three kids. You may say radically "No" if you are tempted to go out with friends when your husband arrives at home. But perhaps you will agree to spend this time praying alone. And both proposals can be temptations, if they are a refuge where you hide from loving and accepting your husband. As

Ignatius of Loyola says, the devil comes cloaked as an "angel of light." At first he will suggest good and holy thoughts and then little by little he strives to gain his own ends by drawing the soul into his hidden deceits.

The first temptation is about stones and bread, and it is related to the meaning of Christ's mission. The devil invites Jesus to work a miracle: "Give us bread, give us a proof of your divinity, of your power, and we will believe." Jesus accepts the challenge; bread is important, but we don't live on bread alone, like the animals. "Bread is important, freedom is more important, but the most important thing is the constant faithfulness and the never failed adoration" (Alfred Delp). Jesus helps us to understand what is really important in our life, in our daily schedule. He will not transform the stones into bread because he himself is the Bread of Life and he will offer himself as nourishment for all of us.

After this first failure, the devil tried to impose on Jesus the conditions of his revelation. "You are right, we need the word of God; since he takes care of us, throw yourself from this height and he will save you." The devil wants Jesus to test God, to treat God as his servant. The same temptation will come later, at the Cross: If you are the son of God, come down from the Cross now, and we will believe in you (see Mt 27:42). But Christ does not test God. He trusts in the Lord, his Father, and he goes to the Cross and the Tomb. This choice is the mystery of trust and obedience. What Adam destroyed in the Paradise through distrust, Jesus begins to restore in the desert through obedience.

The third temptation is the devil's last opportunity. "With other men this temptation worked perfectly. Let us try." Then he offers Jesus the path of the world: power, good opinion, prestige. "Adore me and you will be king and Lord of the world." The devil tries to go against reality; as a creature, he should adore his Creator. But, since he does not know who Jesus is, he asks Christ, the Son of God, to worship him! This time, Jesus' s answer comes quickly and direct: "Get away, Satan!" Jesus has not come into the world to conquer power and dominion. "He emptied himself" through his Incarnation and he will humble himself, becoming obedient to death, even death on a cross (see Phil 2:7–8). His kingdom does not belong to this world (see Jn 18:36).

(3) *Life is a combat: two flags, two standards*

In his Spiritual Exercises, Saint Ignatius of Loyola offers a meditation called: "The two flags." He invites us to imagine a battle between two kings: Jesus and the devil. Each leader calls men to follow him and his way of life. The devil follows the path of the temptations: longing for riches, vain honor of the world, and vast pride (possessions, pleasure, power and prestige). Jesus offers another path: spiritual and even actual poverty, contempt against worldly honor, humility against pride. Jesus offers us a new mind, a new way of thinking, looking, hearing, judging, smiling, crying...

The path offered by Jesus is the path of his life. Jesus enjoyed the bread with his friends and the honor of being called "Rabbi." But his whole existence was in poverty and humility. Riches, honor, and power are good. But when we are with Jesus, under the eyes of the Father, everything receives a new light. It is better to be poor with Christ than rich without him; it is better to be humiliated with Christ than honored without him; it is better to be humble with Christ than proud without him.

The tradition of the Church has developed and condensed this desire of following Christ in the three vows of the religious life: poverty, chastity, and obedience. As Christ was poor, virgin, and obedient, the consecrated wants to experience the treasure of poverty, the fruitfulness of virginity, and the freedom of obedience.

For your prayer

Pray with Saint Ignatius of Loyola. Ask for this new heart and new mind brought by Christ. If you are courageous enough, you can offer your self praying this challenging text of Saint Ignatius. Be courageous. Do not be afraid. God will be always more generous than you. "Surrender to God, and he will do everything for you" (see Ps 37:7).

Eternal Lord of all things, I make my oblation with Thy favor and help, in the presence of Thy infinite Goodness and in the presence of Thy glorious Mother and of all the Saints of the heavenly Court; that I want and desire, and it is my deliberate determination, if only it be Thy greater service and praise, to imitate Thee in bearing all injuries and all abuse and all poverty of spirit, and actual poverty, too, if Thy most Holy Majesty wants to choose and receive me to such life and state (Saint Ignatius).

THE TEMPTATIONS: OUR COMPANION OFFERS US A NEW HEART

(FIRST WEEK OF LENT)

First Sunday of Lent (B)

GOSPEL: MK 1:12–15

The Spirit drove Jesus out into the desert, and he remained in the desert for forty days, tempted by Satan. He was among wild beasts, and the angels ministered to him. After John had been arrested, Jesus came to Galilee proclaiming the gospel of God: "This is the time of fulfillment. The kingdom of God is at hand. Repent, and believe in the gospel."

(1) *The Action of the Holy Spirit*

Today's gospel is especially short. Saint Mark's account of the life of Jesus is usually shorter than those of Matthew and Luke. We may hope that a brief gospel will entail a brief homily.

What can we learn from Mark's account of the Temptations of Jesus? Mark does not offer us an explanation of the three temptations. We only see that the Spirit drove Jesus out into the desert and Jesus remained there and was tempted by Satan.

Jesus was driven by the Holy Spirit. In many places of the gospels we find that Jesus was moved by the Spirit to climb the mountain and pray, to praise the Lord...

The Holy Spirit is at work in this time of Lent. We will see him during Easter working wonders through the apostles, but we will find him already during Lent working in Jesus and in us.

At the beginning of this Lent, let us clarify this point. The most important thing will not be our good proposals, our decisions, our choices...but the action of the Holy Spirit in us. He will be our companion during this Lent.

Of course, it will be important that we change our life, but that will be an answer to the action of the Spirit. He is the one who drives us into the desert of this Lent. He is the one who will teach how to pray.

Therefore, this first Sunday of Lent gives us the opportunity of asking the Holy Spirit to be with us, to work in us, to renew us. We can trust in him: he is not lazy, he does not procrastinate. He will do a nice job in us if we open to him the door of our heart.

(2) *"Among wild beasts and angels"*

The love and work of God comes always first. Our freedom is always an answer to his gift. And why is the Spirit driving us into this new Lent? Because he wants us to encounter Christ in the desert.

Saint Mark tells us that in the desert, Jesus "was among wild beasts, and the angels ministered to him." Proper to the human being is to live among wild beasts and angels, between earth and heaven. As the great theologian Hans Urs Von Balthasar pointed out once, this is the place where we are called to live: we are not just earth, dust or ash, but at the same time we live under the heaven. We are not wild beasts but we are very far from being angels (Theodramma, II. The Man in God).

Like us, Jesus—the Son of God the Father—lives between heaven and earth. He has come to share everything with us. He does not speak to us from the outside. He has become one of us and he knows about our joys and struggles. He is one who suffers, enjoys, laughs, cries, speaks and remains silent, is angry and forgives. He has a heart.

(3) *Repent and believe*

"Repent." This is an invitation we shall often hear in Lent. It doesn't mean to just beat our hearts and walk looking at the floor. To repent means letting God transform us, in order to stop thinking that we are the only ones to build our existence. To repent entails to depend on him.

Many prophets before called the people to repent and change their way of life. But today we hear Jesus, the Son of the living God, inviting us to repentance. The Gospel he proclaims to us can be synthesized in one word: "Abbà," "Father." God is our Father, he has sent his Son to reveal us his love and to repent. During this Lent we are called to conversion, that is, to the memory of our dependence on God our Father. We are creatures, we depend on his love. Guided by the Holy Spirit, let us remember our dignity as children of God.

Meditations for Lent

THE TEMPTATIONS: OUR COMPANION OFFERS US A NEW HEART

(FIRST WEEK OF LENT)

First Sunday of Lent (*C*)

GOSPEL: LK 4:1–13

Jesus, full of the Holy Spirit, returned from the Jordan, and was led by the Spirit for forty days in the wilderness, to be tempted by the devil. He ate nothing during those days, and when they were over he was hungry. The devil said to him, "If you are the Son of God, command this stone to become bread." Jesus answered him, "It is written, / 'One does not live by bread alone.'" Then he took him up and showed him all the kingdoms of the world in a single instant. The devil said to him, "I shall give to you all this power and their glory; for it has been handed over to me, and I may give it to whomever I wish. All this will be yours, if you worship me." Jesus said to him in reply, "It is written: / 'You shall worship the Lord, your God, and him alone shall you serve.'" Then he led him to Jerusalem, made him stand on the parapet of the temple, and said to him, "If you are the Son of God, throw yourself down from here, for it is written: / 'He will command his angels concerning you, to guard you,'/ and: / 'With their hands they will support you, lest you dash your foot against a stone.'" Jesus said to him in reply, "It also says, / 'You shall not put the Lord, your God, to the test.'" When the devil had finished every temptation, he departed from him for a time.

(1) *What really counts in my life*

Our path of Lent starts with the great question of our existence: What does really count in my life? This first Sunday we meditate on the mystery of the Temptations. Jesus goes to the desert in order to answer this question for us: What is really important for us?

Bread, all the kingdoms of the world, the protection of the angels… The devil offers Jesus pleasure, power, possessions and prestige. All these things are good, but they are not what really counts in our life. All these things have been created by God for us, but they are not the essence of our life.

What does really count in my life? Bread and wine, a nice house, a big car, good reputation, an important job… They are all good things, but they are not able to fill our heart. Only God is able to satiate the thirst and hunger—the restlessness—of our heart.

The mystery of the Temptations helps us to understand the danger of idolatry. If we don't believe in God and we don't see the gift of our relationships, we will have another idols. As Pope Francis wrote in his first Encyclical, "the opposite of faith is shown to be idolatry" (*Lumen fidei*, 13). In place of faith in God, we worship an idol, into whose face we can look directly and whose origin we know, because it is the work of our own hands: it can be our TV, Facebook, the iPhone, the videogames, our team, even our favorite sport…

Before an idol, there is no risk. The idol will not call us out of our "comfort zone." Idols "have mouths, but they cannot speak" (*Ps* 115:5), or if they speak, they don't hear. As Pope Francis concludes, idols exist "as a pretext for setting ourselves at the centre of reality and worshiping the work of our own hands."

What really matters in my life is the presence of God, who blesses me with many personal relationships in my life. God gave me parents, grandparents and siblings. He gives me a spouse, children, grandchildren, friends… Theoretically, we all understand it is better to live in a smaller house with my family, than to live in a palace alone. What will you do with the house, the car and everything...if nobody is with you?

(2) *The litmus test of our Lent*

Today, like Israel in the desert, we are invited to abandon our idols and find true freedom following Jesus. "Return to me with all your heart." We are called to undertake a journey of true conversion, recognizing our slavery and the presence of idols that keep us far from God, and therefore far from our spouse, our children, siblings...

Lent offers us three gifts in order to abandon our idols: prayer, fasting and almsgiving. These three activities are ways for putting God first and growing in gratitude. But even these three gifts can be transformed into idols if we don't pay attention. We may pray just to be seen, fasting in order to feel superior to others, and give alms to be considered a nice guy.

The litmus test of our prayer, fasting and almsgiving is charity. If my donations make me proud, if my prayer separates me from my spouse, if my fasting makes me angry...then they have become an idol in my life. What shall I do then? Shall I stop praying, fasting and giving alms? The answer of Jesus is clear: do not stop doing this, just purify your intention, change the way you pray, fast and give alms: "When you pray, do not be like the hypocrites... Go to your inner room, close the door, and pray to your Father In secret" (Mat 6: 5)

The fruit of prayer, almsgiving and fasting is my return to the Lord, which implies always to return to my beloved, to my family, to my mission... Pray, fast and give alms so that you can be more grateful, so that you can forgive better, and accept yourself and your family more joyfully.

> "Return to me with your whole heart, with fasting, and mourning. Rend your hearts, not your garments, and return to the Lord, your God, for he is gracious and

> merciful, slow to anger, abounding in steadfast love, and relenting in punishment." (Joel 2:12–13)

(3) *He departed from him for a time. The combat*

The gospel tells us that the devil departed from Jesus "for a time." The devil has been overcome, but he will come again and will try to deceive Jesus. We know this "time" will be the agony in the garden, at Gethsemane.Jesus fought and we will need to fight in this Lent. To abandon idols is a long combat. Lent reminds us that our life is a never-ending war in which the "weapons" of confession, prayer, fasting and almsgiving are used.

Let us embrace today the combat of prayer. We know the many enemies which surround us: distractions, worries, business, boredom, discouragement... But we know Jesus has also embraced this combat. Whenever we pray, he prays for us, he prays in us, and he receives our prayer. "He prays for us as our priest; He prays in us, as our head; He is prayed to by us, as our God. Let us therefore recognize our voices in him, and his voice in us" (Saint Augustine, *Enarrationes in psalmos*, 85, 1).

Monday (*First Week of Lent*)

GOSPEL: MT 25:31–46

Jesus said to his disciples: "When the Son of Man comes in his glory, and all the angels with him, he will sit upon his glorious throne, and all the nations will be assembled before him. And he will separate them one from another, as a shepherd separates the sheep from the goats. He will place the sheep on his right and the goats on his left. Then the king will say to those on his right, 'Come, you who are blessed by my Father. Inherit the kingdom prepared for you from the foundation of the world. For I was hungry and you gave me food, I was thirsty and you gave me drink, a stranger and you welcomed me, naked and you clothed me, ill and you cared for me, in prison and you visited me.' Then the righteous will answer him and say, 'Lord, when did we see you hungry and feed you, or thirsty and give you drink? When did we see you a stranger and welcome you, or naked and clothe you? When did we see you ill or in prison, and visit you?' And the king will say to them in reply, 'Amen, I say to you, whatever you did for one of these least brothers of mine, you did for me.' Then he will say to those on his left, 'Depart from me, you accursed, into the eternal fire prepared for the Devil and his angels. For I was hungry and you gave me no food, I was thirsty and you gave me no drink, a stranger and you gave me no welcome, naked and you gave me no clothing, ill and in prison, and you did not care for me.' Then they will answer and say, 'Lord, when did we see you hungry or thirsty or a stranger or naked or ill or in prison, and not minister to your needs?' He will answer them, 'Amen, I say to you, what you did not do for one of these least ones, you did not do for me.' And these will go off to eternal punishment, but the righteous to eternal life."

(1) *A new mind: the power of humility*

The devil, being a master of falsehood, takes with him a group of demons made up as angels of light and shouts up at the gates of heaven: "Lift up your heads, O gates, and be lifted up, everlasting doors; and the king of glory shall come in." The angels look down and think: "Our king is returning in triumph from the dead!" So they shout back with joy, the refrain from the psalm: "Who is the king of glory?" But then the devil makes a fatal mistake. When the angels of heaven shout, "Who is the king of glory?" he opens his arms and says, "I am!" In that act of arrogance he shows the angels his outstretched palms. There are no wounding marks of the nails. The angels of heaven refuse to let the impostor in (Alan Jones, *Passion for Pilgrimage*).

"Whoever exalts himself will be humbled; but whoever humbles himself will be exalted" (Mt 23:12). In this Lent, Christ wants to give us a new heart and the beginning of this "spiritual surgery" is humility.

We recognize Jesus for his humility. The angels recognize the impostor by two facts: his arrogance and the lack of wounds in his hands. Full of pride, he speaks about himself and thus he reveals he had not suffered and died for us.

When Jesus comes, we recognize him for his humility and his glorious wounds. He does not speak about himself but about the huge love of the Father, the One who sent him. "Look at the Father, to him the glory for ever and ever." At the same time he shows the wounds he endured for us, the signs of the greatest love.

Up is down and down is up. To follow Christ implies to learn this law of his divine love, which is also the law of true human love. To love my spouse and children, to follow my vocation to the priesthood or religious life...implies these two signs: humility and the wounds of love.

First of all, humility. That submission is my joy, and it is complete: "He must increase; I must decrease" (Jn 3:30). The words of Saint John the Baptist reveal the humility of love. Since it is called to be reciprocal, there is no fear.

Secondly, love, as a decision to affirm and help my beloved to grow, implies wounds. What are the wounds of your love? You slept just a few hours nursing your baby and now you cannot sleep because you have to take care of your children. Your spouse is sick and it is already months that you have taken care of him or her. You struggle to forgive a great offense from your spouse or parents, siblings or children. The wrinkles of your face, the lack of sleep... Do not be afraid! All these wounds are glorious wounds, signs of the greatest love.

(2) *Christ in the least brothers*

In today's Gospel, Jesus speaks about the final judgment which will have only one topic: love. Jesus reveals to us today his mysterious presence in the needy, the lonely, the poor... He is so humble that he wants to reveal himself in the least brothers. He loves us so much that he wants that our wounds may also be his. "Whatever you did for one of these least brothers of mine, you did for me" (Mt 25:40).

This final judgment on love will be merciful and demanding. Jesus does not only say: "Because you insulted me, because you laughed at me, because you killed me..." He is more demanding: "Because you gave me no food...you gave me no drink...you gave me no welcome...." Jesus helps us to understand the lack of love revealed in our sins of omission. At the same time his explanation is a source of hope; really, we can welcome Christ, we can visit him, we can care for him, we are contemporary to him!

(3) *Encountering Christ in my daily life*

Blessed Charles de Foucauld, from a noble French family, converted to Catholicism and wanted to follow Jesus in the closest way possible. He wanted to be with Jesus and he understood that "the more I descended, the more I would be with Jesus." So he went to Nazareth and began to imitate the hidden life of Jesus, the humble and poor manual laborer.

You don't need to go so far to encounter Christ. At home and at work, there you have Christ in the least brothers. "I was naked, alone, hungry, thirsty, tired..."

Is this not your father, coming from work? Or are these not your children, naked, dirty, hungry, crying? Is this not your spouse, who needs your tenderness and forgiveness?

For your prayer

Pray with Blessed Charles de Foucauld his "prayer of abandonment," a beautiful prayer that helps us to grow in understanding and awe before the mystery—God, our Father!

Father, I abandon myself into your hands; do with me what you will. Whatever you may do, I thank you; I am ready for all, I accept all. Let only your will be done in me, and in all your creatures. I wish no more than this, O Lord. Into your hands I commend my soul; I offer it to you with all the love of my heart, for I love you, Lord, and so need to give myself, to surrender myself into your hands, without reserve, and with boundless confidence, for you are my Father.

Tuesday (First Week of Lent)

GOSPEL: MT 6:7–15

Jesus said to his disciples: "In praying, do not babble like the pagans, who think that they will be heard because of their many words. Do not be like them. Your Father knows what you need before you ask him.

"This is how you are to pray: Our Father who art in heaven, / hallowed be thy name, / thy kingdom come, / thy will be done, / on earth as it is in heaven. / Give us this day our daily bread; / and forgive us our trespasses, / as we forgive those who trespass against us; / and lead us not into temptation, / but deliver us from evil.

"If you forgive men their transgressions, your heavenly Father will forgive you. But if you do not forgive men, neither will your Father forgive your transgressions."

(1) *A new mind: Father*

In this week of Lent we are considering the new heart Jesus wants to create in us. Today we consider the essence of this new heart which brings to the world a great revolution. Jesus is teaching his disciples—and us—how to pray. This is proper to any master speaking to his disciples. What it is new is the name of God revealed by Jesus: "This is how you are to pray: Our Father..."

We can call God "Father"! We are not supposed to call him: "President, Excellence, Eminence," or even other philosophical names, as Origin, Absolute Goodness, Principle of Movement, Universal Reason... Jesus teaches us the name of God: Father! In the Garden of Gethsemane we will hear him crying: Abbá! Dad! My dear father!

We may think of the Holy Scripture as a progressive revelation of the name of God. The Bible teaches us to call him our Creator, our Lord, our Shepherd, one who takes care of us. Moses will understand that God is Yahweh, the One who is, the One who stays and remains with me. Today, teaching us the Our Father, Jesus fulfills the path of the Old Testament and reveals to us the definitive name of God: Our Father in Heaven.

Therefore, the new heart of the Christian is the heart of a child of God. We live before the Father who sees what is hidden. His gaze gives us peace and serenity.

Father! Do not lose the novelty and surprise of this name. Father! During a long period of her life, Saint Theresa of Avila meditated on the Our Father. With only the first word "Father," she spent several days and weeks of prayer. Father! Is that possible? In the Mass, before this prayer the priest says: "At the Savior's command, and formed by divine teaching, we dare to say..." Who would dare to call God "our Father" otherwise?

(2) *The power of the word of God*

If we call God "our Father," we can ask him whatever we need. Jesus teaches us what we should ask. In the seven petitions of the Our Father, we have everything we may ask and desire.

The first three petitions speak about the Kingdom of God and look at the future: hallowed be thy Name, thy Kingdom come, thy will be done. Transform, O Father, this earth into the place where your will is done, that is, into heaven!

The other four petitions speak about our needs for our pilgrimage: we need food, and especially, we need the Holy Eucharist, the bread of life. We need the forgiveness of our sins, protection against temptations and the deliverance from evil.

With the Our Father Jesus has given us a school for our desires. The heart of a child of God needs to grow in the desire for good things. Through prayer, our desire is purified and grows in goodness. We desire more and more to keep God's Holy Name, the coming of the Kingdom, the will of God, our daily bread, forgiveness...

Today's first reading tells us that this task is the work of God in us. The word of God is like the rain and the snow coming down from the heavens. They do not return there until they have watered the earth, making it fertile and fruitful (see Is 55:10–11). Likewise, the word of God enters into the heart of the believer and makes it fruitful. When we pray, God is working in us, transforming our heart. He is not lazy but diligent and efficient.

(3) *A new mind: forgiveness*

We can think now about one surprising point of the Our Father. Jesus has taught us to invite God to imitate us. "Forgive us our trespasses, as we forgive those who trespass against us." Forgive us as we forgive others! We are asking God to imitate us! How would we dare to say this unless Jesus had commanded us to do so?

Forgive as we forgive. This petition can be a really dangerous prayer: it is so difficult to forgive! But we can pray this challenging prayer because we trust in God's work in us. God is making our ability to forgive possible; he helps us to forgive. Our forgiveness is already God's action in us and with us!

Therefore we can pray with confidence, forgive us...as we forgive.

Forgiveness is something divine. We are called to forgive but we are unable to do it without God. You may have received small or huge offenses. You may have great anger in your heart because the offense is deep and comes from your dearest and beloved, your husband, your wife, your father, your sibling... Forgiveness is not easy at all, but you need to forgive.

Let us begin with a small step: ask the Lord to increase your desire of forgiving. Lord, you know me. You know I need to forgive, but I cannot do this now. Lord, I want to forgive, help me in this long path. Lord, I want to forgive and I know I also need to be forgiven. This can be your first step: I want to forgive, help me. Perhaps soon you will be able to pray for those who offended you: Lord, I want to forgive, bless those who have offended me.

For your prayer

Today pray with special devotion the Our Father. Pray it slowly, reflecting on your petitions.

You may consider also that Jesus has accomplished all these petitions. He has brought the kingdom of the Father, he has done his will, he has given us the bread of life...and particularly, he has forgiven his enemies. Look at Jesus forgiving on the cross: "Father, forgive them, they know not what they do" (Lk 23:34). Look at Mary, forgiving those who are killing her only son, the Son of God! But also look at Saint Stephen, the first martyr, following Christ as a disciple and forgiving those who were stoning him. May these examples help you in your path of forgiveness.

Wednesday (First Week of Lent)

GOSPEL: LK 11:29–32

While still more people gathered in the crowd, Jesus said to them, "This generation is an evil generation; it seeks a sign, but no sign will be given it, except the sign of Jonah. Just as Jonah became a sign to the Ninevites, so will the Son of Man be to this generation. At the judgment the queen of the south will rise with the men of this generation and she will condemn them, because she came from the ends of the earth to hear the wisdom of Solomon, and there is something greater than Solomon here. At the judgment the men of Nineveh will arise with this generation and condemn it, because at the preaching of Jonah they repented, and there is something greater than Jonah here."

(1) *A new mind: the power of contrition*

Nineveh was a city full of injustice, crime, and sin, similar to Sodom and Gomorrah. But God decided to send them Jonah, the prophet and call them to conversion: "Forty days more and Nineveh shall be destroyed." Who knows—God thought—Nineveh may convert and change and I will be able to save it. God gave to the city forty days of Lent. And even if Jonah was not very passionate in his preaching, the city changed. The king covered himself with sackcloth, sat in the ashes, and proclaimed a long fast: "Who knows, God may relent and forgive."

Nineveh was a city full of injustice, crime, and sin, but their inhabitants decided not to be like Sodom or Gomorrah. Through their sin they were destroying each other, but they heard the voice of the Lord. And the Lord heard the powerful voice of humility and conversion. "A contrite heart you will not spurn." The All-powerful was "obedient" to them because he cannot do anything against the poor and needy. You remember why: "because whatever you did to one of these least brothers…" When we are humble before him, the Father recognizes his Son in us!

(2) *God insists because he needs you*

The new life and heart came to Nineveh through the voice of Jonah. The prophet tried to escape from his vocation. He did not want to go to Nineveh and was reluctant to pray for conversion. He was lukewarm and he wanted a comfortable life, so he escaped far away. But God is more insistent and searched for him: "I want you to be my prophet, my disciple."

In today's Gospel, Jesus proclaims: "There is something greater than Jonah and Solomon here." He is speaking about himself. We can think that this is not very difficult: Solomon was very wise but in the last years of his life he was far from God. And Jonah is not precisely a model of a good life. He is a prophet escaping from his vocation. God almost "persecuted" him until he obtained his acceptance. And still Jonah is lukewarm: he preaches without conviction, without real desire, and he will be angry with God when the whole city is forgiven!

Even in his poverty and tepidity, Jonah becomes a sign of Christ. The "sign of Jonah" is Christ dead and risen on the third day, like Jonah stayed for three days in the belly of the large fish.

The sign of Jonah is also the sign of God looking for his chosen one, for his prophet. There is a great project for Jonah. Even if he tries to escape, God has a great desire: he needs him!

(3) *The sign of Jonah in our daily life*

In today's Gospel, Jesus says that this generation will only receive one sign: the sign of Jonah. We know this is the sign of God searching for his chosen one and especially, this is the sign of the Paschal mystery of Christ, dead and risen on the third day.

In our daily life we also receive the sign of Jonah. In our marriage, in our vocation, in the life of the priest...we also recognize this sign. After three days of Jonah in the belly of the fish—after his "death"—he will return to his mission. The sign of Jonah is the grain of wheat that has to die in order to give life. In our family we experience this law of love: up is down, down is up. To love implies to die to one's self. The logic of love is that my beloved is my priority. I am happy to offer myself—my time, my rest, my work, my health, my money, my hobbies—in order to help him/ her. How many days of suffering and forgiveness under the sign of Jonah! Sacrifice is the test of love.

For your prayer

Today I invite you to repeat the prayer with Psalm 51 of the last week. Like the prophet Nathan with David, Jonah comes to Nineveh, comes to you. It is the time of grace and conversion!

After an intense act of acknowledging the presence of God, pray Psalm 51 asking for forgiveness.

If you have problems in your relationship with your spouse, parents, children...you can ask the Lord: Forgive.

Thursday (First Week of Lent)

GOSPEL: MT 7:7–12

Jesus said to his disciples: "Ask and it will be given to you; seek and you will find; knock and the door will be opened to you. For everyone who asks, receives; and the one who seeks, finds; and to the one who knocks, the door will be opened. Which one of you would hand his son a stone when he asked for a loaf of bread, or a snake when he asked for a fish? If you then, who are wicked, know how to give good gifts to your children, how much more will your heavenly Father give good things to those who ask him.

"Do to others whatever you would have them do to you. This is the law and the prophets."

(1) *A new mind: the power of prayer*

"Ask and it will be given to you" (Mt 7:7). Today, Jesus is very clear: Ask, seek, knock... and it will be given to you, you will find the door will be opened to you. Jesus is inviting—almost commanding us—to ask the Lord with confidence and insistence. In the prayer of petition we proclaim at the same time our need and our faith in God's power and mercy. We ask because we need; we ask because we know God is powerful enough to help us; we ask because we know God is merciful and wants our growth, our happiness, and our fruitfulness; he will not give us a snake or a stone. So let us ask, seek, and knock! We will proclaim our poverty and God's greatness. This relationship is the power of prayer.

But if Jesus is inviting us to ask, why don't we soon receive what we ask for? Sometimes we ask for a grace and it seems we don't receive it. Why?

God knows very well—much better than us—our needs, and we don't know how to pray. If we ask him for a loaf of bread or a fish he will not hand us a stone or a snake. And if we ask him for stones and snakes, he will not hand us them. So many times, we don't know what is really better for us; but God knows.

And perhaps we don't receive what we ask for because we are not asking well. We ask for really good things but we don't ask with our whole heart, with perseverance and true faith. We don't ask like Queen Esther does. Today's first reading shows us a model of prayer of petition.

First of all, Queen Esther is not asking for herself but for the whole people of Israel, spread in different cities of the Persian Empire. Haman the Agagite, a powerful vizier of King Xerxes Ahasuerus of Persia will prepare a plot against the Jews. Out of hatred for a Jewish servant, Mordecai, who for his faith refuses to render him homage, Haman will try to kill all the Jews living there. Esther, niece and adopted daughter of Mordecai, was chosen queen by King Xerxes, and now she will have to risk her life in order to save the people of Israel. When you ask, ask especially for others. Of course, you can ask for yourself, but pay special attention to the needs of the others.

Secondly, in her petition Esther will risk her life. She will have to go to the king without being summoned. This implies automatic penalty of death, unless the king extends to her the golden scepter, thus sparing her life. In order to do that, Esther will pray and ask for prayers. She will ask Mordecai, her adoptive father: "Go and assemble all the Jews who are in Susa; fast on my behalf, all of you, not eating or drinking night or day for three days. I and my maids will also fast in the same way. Thus prepared, I will go to the king, contrary to the law. If I perish, I perish!" (Est 4:16).

Learn from Esther's courage. She is the strong woman who will speak with "the Lion," the great king. She is taking her life in her hand in order to save her people. "Put in my mouth persuasive words in the presence of the lion" (Est 4:24). This prayer is the new mind which will be fulfilled in Christ; when you ask for God's help, offer your life. Take your life in your hand! Have you ever done this? Offer your life to the Lord without reserve.

(2) *Ask so that your desire grows*

King Xerxes heard Esther's petition and reversed his royal decree of extermination. If the "lion" heard her petition, what about God, our Father? Is he going to deny us what we need? But we may still object something against prayer. When we ask God we acknowledge he is Almighty and Good. But God, not only can do everything and wants every good for us, but also knows everything. If he knows what I need, why should I ask anything? Is he perhaps ignorant about my poverty and needs? Do I have to remind him?

Saint Augustine gave us an answer to this objection. We ask the Lord because prayer is the "gym of our desire." Through petition we grow in our good desires. I ask God to give me fortitude and humility, and thus I grow in my desire of these virtues. I ask the Lord to bless my husband, and thus I grow in love and tenderness toward him... Through petition, I develop the good desires of my heart and I understand better what is important in my life.

Think again about Esther. Before her great petition she was a good friend of God who had received the gift of being queen. Through her intercession before the King, she grew in wisdom, patience, and love for her people and gratitude to God. Also for her, prayer was the "gym of her desires."

(3) *The sign of Esther: God desires to show his generosity*

If yesterday we considered the sign of Jonah and the power of contrition, today we can consider the sign of Esther and the power of our prayer of petition. The foundation of our prayer is the generosity of God. As Angelo Silesio wrote: "God is great. He likes to grant great gifts to us. The problem is our heart, which is too small to receive them." God wants to share his joy with us.

Esther is a sign for us: she shows the beauty of prayer when we ask for others. She manifests the amazing power of prayer when we offer our lives together with our petition: Put in my mouth your words.

For your prayer

Offer yourself with Queen Esther, who asked the Lord and obtained the salvation of her people. Today you can pray with the servant of God, Msgr. García Lahiguera, bishop of Valencia, Spain. He speaks about priesthood, but his prayer can be applied also to family life. Queen Esther understood this very well: she took her life in her hand. She did not reserve herself.

To reserve oneself: what an anti-priestly word!

To reserve myself? For whom? Am I not wholly yours and only yours, Lord?

To reserve myself? What for? Is not this and now your complete will?

To reserve myself? For when? Do I have any other time, save this which I am now living?

Do not forget these words: every great work—holiness—is the fruit of a great passion, love, at the service of a great ideal: Christ. Do not forget that the measure of love is to love without measure.

Friday (First Week of Lent)

GOSPEL: MT 5:20–26

Jesus said to his disciples: "I tell you, unless your righteousness surpasses that of the scribes and Pharisees, you will not enter into the Kingdom of heaven.

"You have heard that it was said to your ancestors, You shall not kill; and whoever kills will be liable to judgment. But I say to you, whoever is angry with his brother will be liable to judgment, and whoever says to his brother, Raqa, will be answerable to the Sanhedrin, and whoever says, 'You fool,' will be liable to fiery Gehenna. Therefore, if you bring your gift to the altar, and there recall that your brother has anything against you, leave your gift there at the altar, go first and be reconciled with your brother, and then come and offer your gift. Settle with your opponent quickly while on the way to court. Otherwise your opponent will hand you over to the judge, and the judge will hand you over to the guard, and you will be thrown into prison. Amen, I say to you, you will not be released until you have paid the last penny."

(1) *A new mind: the power of meekness*

The Gospels show us Jesus' anger on different occasions. Jesus was not weak nor shy, but strong and bold. Remember him in the temple of Jerusalem, cleansing it from all the business—buying and selling—that was transforming the house of the Father into a den of thieves (see Mk 11:15–19). He even overturned the tables of the money changers. Saint John adds that he made a whip out of cords and drove all from the temple courts, both sheep and cattle! (see John 2:13–16). This is not the weak and over sweet Jesus we sometimes imagine.

There is in us a good wrath, a good anger, which is a human passion against what is wrong or evil. If someone tries to kill my family, my beloved, for instance, I will be angry and react with wrath, protecting them. But to be honest, our anger is not usually holy or good, but it is a complaint against my brother, against what I cannot understand. Today Jesus invites us to take away from our lives any anger against our "brother," that is, against our spouse, father, siblings, children…

This meekness is what Jesus wants us to learn from his heart. Think about this: The Gospels have only left us one moment in which Jesus, the Master, said to his disciples: "Learn from me." Of course during his life, he offers his life as a path for his disciples, like when he washed their feet: I have done this, so that you do the same. But only once we hear the Lord saying: "Learn from me." When this happened, Christ did not call us to imitate him "in general": learn from my intelligence, fortitude, generosity, joy, prudence, patience…. He rather chose two special virtues of his heart: "Learn from me, for I am meek and humble of heart" (Mt 11:29).

Meekness and humility. This attitude is the secret power of the heart of Christ. Meekness does not mean weakness or lack of energy, but rather, a different kind of courage and boldness. Jesus knows that he is always with the Father, who sees what is secret. Therefore he understands the Father has a plan, a time, a rhythm for his life. Instead of anger, he answers with the trust and confidence of the Son.

(2) *Do not be afraid of your anger*

To not be afraid of your anger is easy to say but difficult to do. How can I overcome my anger? Is that really possible? In the second half of the nineteenth century, a young Italian priest called Giuseppe Sarto was in his parish with his sister. One evening he was suffering a really bad toothache and he was complaining aloud. His sister criticized him: "You are weak, you are always complaining..." Then Fr. Giuseppe, full of anger, slapped her in the face. Some years later, Fr. Giuseppe became a bishop, a cardinal, and later even pope. Today we know him as Saint Pius X.

Of course Saint Pius X was not a saint because of this slap. You can imagine that the same day, he apologized to his sister about that. Fr. Giuseppe was aware of his anger, and with the grace of God, fought against it and step by step overcame it.

Do not be afraid of your anger. You can still be a saint. Ask for forgiveness and ask for self-knowledge, which is the first step toward conversion. Lord, help me to know myself and to acknowledge I need your help. Remember the words of Saint Paul: "Be angry but do not sin; do not let the sun set on your anger, and do not leave room for the devil" (Eph 4:26–27). If you are angry and you have talked again with your spouse, do not let the sun set on your anger, but go and ask forgiveness: I am sorry. Forgive me.

(3) *The sign of my brother*

"Go first and be reconciled with your brother!" (Mt 5:24). Today we receive the sign of our brother, which is a sacred one. Perhaps you are coming to Mass or Adoration, but you are not forgiving your husband, your daughter...for whatever reason. Jesus invites you to leave your gift there at the altar, go, and be reconciled. It is good you came to the Adoration chapel, but do not look for a refuge there. You came to Christ and he is now sending you to your home: Go and be reconciled with your "brother," that is, your spouse, children, parents...

Being reconciled with your brother is being reconciled with God. Let us consider this: when anger comes to my heart and I complain about someone, I am complaining about this presence in my life. We can say that at the end, I am complaining against God, who has created this person and has given him to me as husband, wife, child...

Why do I complain? Cruel judgments made in anger come from my lack of humility and meekness. I want to be the judge and decide what makes sense and what does not make sense in my life. I complain because I do not recognize the presence and action of God in this person: my spouse, my friend... Today pray to the Father: Lord, you know better. Give me humility to accept what I do not understand. Help me to see your hand and your providence in the persons I encounter everyday, especially my spouse, children, parents, siblings, coworkers... You know better. Help me to enter into your project. Help me to understand the sense of everyone in my life.

For your prayer

Today you can ask the Lord to give you and your family the virtues of his heart: humility and meekness. You can use a part of the "serenity prayer," written by Reinhold Niebuhr (1892–1971) and that was adopted by Alcoholics Anonymous.

God, grant me the serenity to accept the things I cannot change, the courage to change the things I can, and wisdom to know the difference.

Saturday (First Week of Lent)

GOSPEL: MT 5:43–48

Jesus said to his disciples: "You have heard that it was said, You shall love your neighbor and hate your enemy. But I say to you, love your enemies, and pray for those who persecute you, that you may be children of your heavenly Father, for he makes his sun rise on the bad and the good, and causes rain to fall on the just and the unjust. For if you love those who love you, what recompense will you have? Do not the tax collectors do the same? And if you greet your brothers only, what is unusual about that? Do not the pagans do the same? So be perfect, just as your heavenly Father is perfect."

(1) *The surprise of forgiveness*

If you have read *Les misérables* of Victor Hugo (or perhaps you have watched one of the movies or the musical), you will remember its great beginning. Jean Valjean steals a loaf of bread for his family and spends nineteen oppressive years in prison. After finishing his term, he is released a hardened man and receives a yellow card, a document which will remind everybody he is a dangerous person. He arrives to a village where nobody wants to offer him food or a room for rest. It is cold winter and he tries to find an empty barn to sleep, but even the dogs do not welcome him. After four days and nights walking, someone tells him: "Go to the square, to the house of the bishop, perhaps there you will find something." In the square there is a door always open and behind it a not very welcoming woman, the bishop's sister. When this lady is about to expel Jean, they hear the voice of an old man, the voice of the bishop. Bishop Myriel of Digne, France, welcomes Jean, asks his sister to prepare the best meal with the best silver and gives Jean a room and a comfortable bed. During the night the temptation comes again; Jean gets up in silence, and he puts the silver in his bag. When he is about to leave, the bishop—hearing the noise—comes from his room: "What's going on? Who's there?" Full of anxiety, Jean hits the bishop and runs away.

The following day, the bishop's sister spends hours complaining: "I told you! We should have not trusted in this man! And now our silver is gone and you have these bad wounds on your head, and it is your fault. At least we still have the silver candlesticks!" An hour later someone knocks at the door; the local police have caught Jean Valjean with the stolen silver.

Silence. The bishop, with a wonderful headache, looks at the silver, at the police, and at Jean. "So here you are! Thanks to God you are here. You forgot to take the candlesticks, which were also my gift." In these few seconds the world is recreated. The bishop explains to the police: "Thank you, sir, for bringing back this fellow man! This silver is my gift to him." Surprised by the news, the police leave the house, and Jean remains in front of the bishop, conquered and transformed by the power of forgiveness. The whole book—more than five hundred pages—will be the development of Jean's life and how this encounter renews his whole life. This transformation is the power of forgiveness. It surprises us and opens an unexpected novelty in our life.

(2) *The mind of Christ: love your enemies, pray for them*

"Love those who love you and hate those who hate you." This saying is what we usually think of as "natural" and "human." I give to you because you have given to me; I give to you so that you might give to me. This law is already something positive. At least, it helps us to understand that we are not called to hate those who love us. We find this law in the Old Testament as a progress in humanity: "Eye for an eye; tooth for a tooth" (see Ex 21:23–25; Lev 24:18–20). If someone kills your donkey, you may kill his donkey, but nothing else (lex talionis). The biblical counsel of retaliation—present also in other cultures, as in the famous Code of Hammurabi—was already a step forward toward love: the punishment corresponds in kind and degree to the injury. Before that, there was no law but just an unreasonable reaction, such as the response of Lamech, one of the descendants of Cain: "I have killed a man for wounding me, / a young man for bruising me. / If Cain is avenged seven times, / then Lamech seventy-seven times" (Gn 4:23–24).

But it is not enough just to love those who love us. As Martin Luther King, Jr. said, "the old law of an eye for an eye leaves everyone blind." What can we do then? Today Jesus offers us something more natural and human than this, something divine. We discover this "more" in Christ's life. He loves those who love him, like Lazarus, his friend, or Mary, his mother. But Christ also loves his enemies, the Pharisees, and tries to transform their hearts. Consider also what happens on the Cross: "Father, forgive them, for they know not what they do" (Lk 23:34). Jesus prays and intercedes for his enemies! He also forgives Peter, who denied him three times. This forgiveness is the path opened to us by Christ, and it is the greatest proof of love. As Saint Paul says, the proof of the love of God is that while we were still sinners—his enemies—Christ died for us (see Rom 5: 8–10) so that we may become his friends.

Let me tell you something else: this great love is not anti-human or anti-natural, but on the contrary, it is the revelation of the highest human love. Jesus shows us with his life the goal of our love: we are called to love in a divine way, which is the fulfillment of our humanity. Anger, hatred, revenge, and resentment against the enemy are not truly human.

Forgiveness is something divine. Sometimes, complete forgiveness and reconciliation on earth are not possible. The other has died long time ago, or I am walking in my desire for forgiveness and my heart needs more time to heal the deep wounds. In this case, hopefully, if we are faithful to the Lord, we will embrace our enemy in heaven, when we will encounter each other, purified from any sin and in the presence of the Lord.

(3) *The power of love: enemies transformed into friends*

Following the example of Jesus, we are called to love our enemies and transform them into friends. If the bishop of Digne was able to forgive, it was thanks to the power of Jesus on the cross. The reason to love our enemies is this hope—that they will become our friends. Christ loves and forgives those who are killing him. Of course, he does not love them "because they are killing him," but because he wants to transform their hearts and call them to conversion. Jesus loves Peter, even when he is denying him three times. He does not love Peter "because he is lying," but because Jesus wants to move the disciple to repentance and a new life.

"I do not have enemies," you may think. "Nobody wants to kill me and I don't desire the death of any person." That is ok, but perhaps you try to ignore this person, your husband, your coworker... Ignoring is a way of hating. As Mother Teresa of Calcutta said about the poor people who were starving: "They don't die for hunger; they die for indifference." Our omission can be a way of hating.

But in any case, we all have enemies. Jesus had enemies. My enemies are those who desire my evil, those who are not helping me to be saint; they desire my sin or my failure. Sometimes they are not real enemies, but I see them as enemies. It happens, perhaps, with my parents when they don't let me do what I would like to or when they correct me.

The first of all these enemies is myself. In my heart there is a battle; God dwells there, but the evil wants to conquer some parts of my life. The enemies are usually at home. I can look at my brother or my husband as my enemy because he doesn't want what I want, he doesn't reject what I reject. My enemies are also those who love me in a bad way, those who do not forgive me: my husband or my children. If I don't act quickly, this opposition will generate hatred and will ask for retaliation. It happens the same with the water of the river when it remains stagnant and it corrodes. We enter then in the dynamic of revenge; you did it to me, so I have right to do the same...

What is Jesus doing? He loves his enemies in order to transform them into friends. If he addresses the Pharisees with hard words, it is in order to change their hearts. On the cross, Jesus will conquer the heart of one of the thieves, who is crucified with him: "Jesus, remember me when you come into your kingdom" (Lk 23:42). And Jesus will also gain the heart of the Roman soldier.

FROM ASH TO WATER

As Jesus did, I can love my spouse, children, parents...and transform them again into friends. If in these last weeks, months, or years, I am far from my spouse, it is the moment to begin again and to rebuild our relationship through forgiveness. Don't lose this hope. Don't leave room to resentment. Every night, before you go to bed, pray for your spouse and, when you are prepared, ask your spouse to forgive you.

Our heavenly Father "makes his sun rise on the bad and the good, and causes rain to fall on the just and the unjust" (Mt 5:45). This generosity is a great mystery of patience. Jesus does not want to say that everything —justice or injustice, good or evil—is ok. He reveals the great patience of our Father, who waits until this transformation of the enemies into friends is finished. We know well that, on the last day, when Jesus will come, he will separate the just from the unjust, the good from the evil.

But what happens when the one who offended me can offend others? To forgive him, does this imply that I cannot seek justice and prevent this person from hurting others? True forgiveness implies that I try to desire the best for my enemy. What is the best for this person that has hurt me? Free from hatred, forgiveness will imply to seek the conversion of my enemy and this implies to seek justice: that he may repent and understand the path of evil and the lie in which he is right now. If someone steals from us or kills a friend or a relative of ours, if someone abuses us in different ways, we are called to seek justice so that this person may not steal, kill, or abuse anymore and may repair the harm he has caused. Forgiveness, mercy, truth, and justice are not enemies but the best friends! "Love and truth will meet; / justice and peace will kiss. / Truth will spring from the earth; / justice will look down from heaven" (Ps 85:11–12).

For your prayer

Today pray with Saint Francis. Through forgiveness you can become an instrument of his peace: in your family and at work, wherever you go.

Lord, make me an instrument of your peace; where there is hatred, let me sow love. Where there is injury, pardon; where there is error, truth; where there is doubt, faith; where there is despair, hope; where there is darkness, light; and where there is sadness, joy. O Divine Master, grant that I may not so much seek to be consoled as to console, to be understood as to understand, to be loved as to love. For it is giving that we receive, it is in pardoning that we are pardoned, and it is in dying that we are born to eternal life.

THE TRANSFIGURATION: OUR HOPE

(SECOND WEEK OF LENT)

Second Sunday of Lent (A)

GOSPEL: MT 17:1–9

Jesus took Peter, James, and John his brother, and led them up a high mountain by themselves. And he was transfigured before them; his face shone like the sun and his clothes became white as light. And behold, Moses and Elijah appeared to them, conversing with him.

Then Peter said to Jesus in reply, "Lord, it is good that we are here. If you wish, I will make three tents here, one for you, one for Moses, and one for Elijah." While he was still speaking, behold, a bright cloud cast a shadow over them, then from the cloud came a voice that said, "This is my beloved Son, with whom I am well pleased; listen to him." When the disciples heard this, they fell prostrate and were very much afraid. But Jesus came and touched them, saying, "Rise, and do not be afraid." And when the disciples raised their eyes, they saw no one else but Jesus alone.

As they were coming down from the mountain, Jesus charged them, "Do not tell the vision to anyone until the Son of Man has been raised from the dead."

(1) *Jesus wants to reveal his mystery*

During the last week we have deepened in the new mind and heart brought by Jesus. To follow him implies to assume our cross and be with him, following his footprints. Now we begin our second week of Lent with Jesus again on the mountain. He was really a mountain-lover! Christ was amazed before the great horizons you can see from the top of a mountain. He loved the silence and peace after the effort of climbing.

On Mount Tabor we see Christ revealing something new. Jesus is not only one like us, tempted like we are tempted. Today, he is going to reveal his glory. In his radiant face we will understand that he is not only our brother, but also our Lord, the Lord of heaven and earth. He is the foundation of our hope.

We don't know exactly what happened there. The Gospels say that Jesus "was transfigured before them." Transfiguration means a change in the appearance, a "metamorphosis." According to Saint Thomas Aquinas, this was the greatest miracle of Jesus. Matthew explains that Jesus' face shone like the sun and his clothes were white as light. Mark specifies that the color of his clothes—a dazzling white—was not a natural color, but something extraordinary, "white, such as no fuller on earth could bleach them" (Mk 9:3). The radiant light of his face and clothes is a sign of the great work of the Holy Spirit in Jesus' heart.

Jesus does not reveal his glory to the crowd but just to three of the disciples, who are chosen to witness this moment. Christ takes Peter, James, and John with him and they climb Mount Tabor in a moment of intimacy in which they better understand Jesus' identity. The disciples had seen Jesus sleeping, eating, resting, walking…as a normal man, and they had seen him working wonders and miracles, and speaking as nobody had ever spoken. Who was Jesus? One of us, the son of Mary, but at the same time, one very different from us: the Son of God. To confirm this revelation, the disciples will hear the testimony of God the Father: "This is my beloved Son, with whom I am well pleased; listen to him" (Mt 17:5).

Look at Christ; he is one of us. And Jesus, our brother, is the Creator of the world! We need these two elements to understand Jesus and the solid foundations of our hope: if he were only our Lord in heaven, he would be very far, and if he were only one of us, he could not save us. Look at him; he has a human face, and in his face, his eyes, his nose, his mouth, you can see the Creator and Savior of the World. He wants to tell you who he is! Choose us, Lord, to go with you to the holy mountain; reveal to us your glory.

(2) *Jesus, the fulfillment of the promises*

But together with the three disciples, Jesus, the light of the Spirit, and the voice of the Father, we also have two witnesses. Moses and Elijah appeared to them, conversing with Jesus. For us it is difficult to understand the meaning of this fact. Moses and Elijah were two great friends of God and heroes in the story of Israel.

Moses established the covenant with God on Mount Sinai. After his encounters with God, his face was shining so powerfully that he had to cover it, in order to speak to his people. For Moses this encounter is awesome. You may remember (otherwise you can refresh your memory reading the end of the Exodus) that Moses died before entering the promised land. So, the Transfiguration of Jesus was the first time he was there. And here Moses understands that the promise of God is not just a land with milk and honey, but a Person. He is before the Promised Land, Jesus Christ, the place where we can rest and rejoice. In him the covenant of God with Israel—all his promises and his law—have been accomplished!

And what about Elijah? Elijah was a prophet and a wonder-worker in the ninth century BC. He was persecuted because he defended the worship of Yahweh over the Phoenician god Baal and the idols. During his life, he brought fire down from the sky through his prayer, he raised the dead, and worked great miracles. Finally he did not die, but was taken up in a whirlwind, accompanied by a chariot and horses. Why is he here now with Jesus?

According to the book of the prophet Malachi, Elijah would return "before the day of the LORD comes, / the great and terrible day" (Mal 3:23). So the Christ would have no power until Elijah comes again to anoint him. We know that Jesus was asked about this coming on another occasion and he answered: "I tell you that Elijah has already come, and they did not recognize him but did to him whatever they pleased.... Then the disciples understood that he was speaking to them of John the Baptist" (Mt 17:12–13). On Mount Tabor, Elijah speaks with Jesus, who is the origin of all his wonders and he testifies that Jesus Christ is the true God, the Creator of the world.

Therefore, Moses and Elijah come to testify that Christ is the fulfillment of the Scriptures and of the whole creation. God is faithful to his promises. And what about the promises of your life? What has God promised to you on the day of your baptism, first communion, confirmation, wedding...? Today we are called to remember the promises of God to us. He keeps his word!

(3) *Our transfiguration*

"Lord, it is good that we are here. I will make three tents here, one for you, one for Moses, and one for Elijah" (Mt 17:4). One of the most tender and funny moments of the Gospel is this experience. On Mount Tabor, Peter is in heaven and he wants to stay. In order to remain there he has an idea: let us make three tents. He does not think about a tent for himself and the other disciples; he does not realize Jesus, Moses, and Elijah don't need any tent. He just wants to stay there because "it is good that we are here!" He has this experience of heaven in the middle of his life.

Sometimes we think that heaven is just something that will come after death. And we think that our task in this "earthly life," in this "valley of tears" is just to suffer, endure, and offer our sad and painful life. Heaven will come later; now we have sufferings and sufferings... It is true that human life has an important ingredient of bearing our cross. We are pilgrims walking toward our homeland. Christian life helps us to love more, which always implies a greater vulnerability; we suffer more because we love more. But our life on earth is not called to be just a dark valley. As a good friend, Jesus wants us to enjoy this life. We can also remember how Jesus enjoyed the peaceful years in Nazareth with Mary and Joseph, the discussions and potluck evenings in Bethany, the quiet moments with the disciples...

Heaven is not just something of the future. On Mount Tabor, the three disciples experienced a foretaste of the joy and peace of heaven. Heaven, that is, life eternal—our friendship with God—begins here, in our daily life, in our family, in our work. In the middle of the tasks and movements of our life, we can recognize several moments of transfiguration: it is this dinner alone with my spouse, this time of adoration as a family, or my daily mass... But also we have those very special moments of glory in our pilgrimage: a child is born, our son is baptized, our daughter receives her first communion, our oldest daughter gets married, we celebrate four, nine, twenty, or fifty years of marriage.

But don't be tempted. "It is good that we are here," but now we must go down, to our daily life. This mystery is a reminder of the beauty of our life and of our destiny, our resurrection. But now your mission is not to remain here. If you are married, you are called to be holy as spouse, mother or father, not as a nun or a monk. You have been transfigured, but now go down and bring to the world the face of Christ, his glory.

For your prayer

Today I invite you to make a visit to Jesus present in the Tabernacle. If you can, you may go to the Adoration Chapel and stay for a few minutes. His real presence is our Mount Tabor, our solace, and our hope. You can stay remembering the presence of the Lord and giving thanks because he has come, not as a tourist, but to stay with us. "Lord, it is good that we are here." Remain with us, do not go.

Perhaps it is time for the second confession of Lent or for a first one if you have not been able to come until now. Do not be afraid. You still have time to begin again in this Lent. Today, Jesus in Mount Tabor wants to remind you of the beauty of your vocation.

Second Sunday of Lent (B)

GOSPEL: MK 9: 2–10

Jesus took Peter, James, and John and led them up a high mountain apart by themselves. And he was transfigured before them, and his clothes became dazzling white, such as no fuller on earth could bleach them. Then Elijah appeared to them along with Moses, and they were conversing with Jesus. Then Peter said to Jesus in reply, "Rabbi, it is good that we are here! Let us make three tents: one for you, one for Moses, and one for Elijah." He hardly knew what to say, they were so terrified. Then a cloud came, casting a shadow over them; from the cloud came a voice, "This is my beloved Son. Listen to him." Suddenly, looking around, they no longer saw anyone but Jesus alone with them.

As they were coming down from the mountain, he charged them not to relate what they had seen to anyone, except when the Son of Man had risen from the dead. So they kept the matter to themselves, questioning what rising from the dead meant.

(1) *"Let there be light!"*

The mystery of Transfiguration is a mystery of light. At the beginning of creation, God created light. "'Fiat lux'—let there be light!" (Gn 1:2). Like the other creatures, light is a sign that reveals something of God. We could say that light is a reflection of his glory. When God appears, his brightness is "like the light, rays flashed from his hand" (Hebrews 3:3). According to the Psalms (104:2), light is the mantle with which God covers himself.

The revelation of the light will be accomplished in Jesus Christ. He comes as the light of the world. "He who follows me will not walk in darkness, but will have the light of life" (Jn 8:12). In Jesus, the light of God illumines definitively human life and the course of history.

In our daily life we know that light brings to us the colors of the world, its shapes and a sense of warm and peace. The sunrise comes with the music of the birds welcoming the gift of light.

In this second week of Lent, we remember the mystery of the Transfiguration. Lent is not a time of darkness but of purifying light. Through our prayer, fasting and almsgiving, Jesus is bringing his light into our lives. When Jesus enters into my life, he brings with him new colors, music, peace… Who believes in Jesus, is able to see and discover the beauty of the world.

(2) *"Such as no fuller on earth could bleach them"*

Saint Mark has expressed this novelty of Christ in a very special way. It was probably saint Peter who mentioned this detail to him. At the moment of the Transfiguration, the clothes of Jesus became dazzling white. As Mark notes, they were white, "such as no fuller on earth could bleach them."

Whenever Jesus is present, there is a sense of something unique. In this case Mark speaks about the dazzling white of Jesus' clothes. In other passages of the gospels we see the people full of awe considering that "nobody was spoken like him" or that "no one worked wonders like those."

Christ brings something completely unexpected into our lives. His light is unique. No other person, no other experience will ever bring a joy like the joy of Christ.

The mystery of Transfiguration is for us a reminder of the gift we have received. When Christ entered into our lives we transfigured us, he gave us new light and hope. Many times our daily struggles, frustrations, resentments. . .prevent us to recognize this light. In this week of Lent we are invited to remember that Christ has come to bring greatness into my life. Remember the transfiguration: your transfiguration: remember your conversion, the times of intense prayer, the moments of deep joy when you met your spouse, when your son was born. . . Many problems come into our lives because we forget our transfiguration, because we live without this mystery. Let us celebrate daily this mystery. Christ reveals his glory to us. His light becomes our light and we shine in the middle of the world.

(3) *Light in advance*

But where is this wonderful light in the middle of our life, in this valley of tears? How can I live this unique joy if I am sick, if I am struggling so much in my family life, at work and everywhere?

Saint Mark gives us a detail of the Transfiguration that helps us to answer this question. The disciples received a commandment of the Lord: they should keep the matter to themselves. This was not a selfish reaction but obedience to Jesus. Keeping all these events in their hearts, the disciples will imitate the wisdom of Mary. Like the mother of Jesus in Nazareth, they will keep all these things, reflecting on them in their hearts (Lk 2:19.51). They will remain silent in the outside, but they will be questioning and trying to understand what happened in mount Tabor.

The Transfiguration is a moment of "light in advance." It is not yet the Resurrection, but an anticipation. In our daily life we experience the joy of the Gospel amid many struggles and weaknesses. On Mount Tabor, Christ prepares his disciples—and prepares us—for the sufferings of the Passion. "When you will see me alone on the Cross, abandoned and despised, remember the bright of my face, remember the dazzling white of my clothes."

Christ prepares me for the future: richness or poverty, health or sickness. "Whenever you find yourself alone on the Cross, abandoned and despised, remember your times of Tranfiguration. We remember the gifts of the past because they speak about the triumph of Christ in the future. This is what Saint Augustine called *memoria futuri*, the memory of the future. Whenever we remember the gift of the beginning we received new hope for the future.

For your prayer

A few years ago, Benedict XVI quoted this beautiful Greek hymn: "*You were transfigured on the mountain and your disciples, insofar as they were able, contemplated your glory, in order that, on seeing you crucified, they would understand that your Passion was voluntary and proclaim to the world that you are truly the splendour of the Father*" (Benedict XVI, 20 March 2011).

Second Sunday of Lent (*C*)

GOSPEL: LK 9: 28B–36

Jesus took Peter, John, and James and went up a mountain to pray. While he was praying his face changed in appearance and his clothing became dazzling white. And behold, two men were conversing with him, Moses and Elijah, who appeared in glory and spoke of his exodus that he was going to accomplish in Jerusalem. Peter and his companions had been overcome by sleep, but becoming fully awake, they saw his glory and the two men standing with him. As they were about to part from him, Peter said to Jesus, "Master, it is good that we are here; let us make three tents, one for you, one for Moses, and one for Elijah." But he did not know what he was saying. While he was still speaking, a cloud came and cast a shadow over them, and they became frightened when they entered the cloud. Then from the cloud came a voice that said, "This is my chosen Son; listen to him." After the voice had spoken, Jesus was found alone. They fell silent and did not at that time tell anyone what they had seen.

(1) *Entering the cloud*

In this second Sunday of Lent, the Lord invites us to go up the mountain to pray with him. Those invited to this hike were only three disciples. Peter, James and John were chosen among the chosen. This fact reveals us that on Mount Tabor Jesus will reveal something very important and something that is very deep in his heart. It will be a mystery of intimacy.

Jesus invites us to climb the mountain to pray with him. Only if we climb the mountain we will "enter the cloud," that is, we will encounter his mystery of love. The mount of Tabor was not a fourteener of Colorado but it was not either a small hill. If you have visited the Holy Land as a pilgrim, you will remember the very narrow roads and the crazy taxis you need to take in order to reach the summit of the mountain. Jesus invites us to climb because the greatest gifts of his heart come together with great effort.

To pray together with your spouse, to gather your family in order to pray during Lent, to stop by your prayer corner at home just for a minute, to visit the adoration chapel... All these decisions are "climbing the mountain" which sometimes imply a great effort. There are always many good reasons to postpone our prayer: the laundry, the TV show, facebook, "we are tired"; "it is late"; "it is too early"...

In a word, the enemy is called "tomorrow." When Saint Augustine writes about his conversion, we describes the situation of his heart when he knew the Lord was knocking at his door. Tomorrow I will open the door, tomorrow. "I sent up these sorrowful words: How long, how long, *tomorrow and tomorrow*? Why not now? Why not is there this hour an end to my uncleanness?" (*Confessions,* chapter 12)

Only when we climb the mountain of the Transfiguration we receive God's light. Saint Luke says that the disciples "entered the cloud," they were surrounded by the mystery of God.

(2) *The revelation from the cloud: the Father*

When they entered the cloud, the three disciples heard a voice from heaven: "This is my chosen Son: listen to him." The disciples were told that Jesus of Nazareth, their *Rabbi,* their Master was the "chosen Son" of God. According to the gospel of Luke, during the Baptism of Jesus, a voice came from heaven proclaiming Jesus as the beloved Son (Lk 3:22) and in the Temptations, the devil will discuss with Jesus: "If you are the Son of God..." (Lk 4:9).

Jesus' mission—the core of the Gospel—can be described in this way: He is the Son of God who comes to reveal to us that God is our Father. The Father is always in his heart, in his memory and in his lips. This is a continuous pattern of Jesus' preaching. During the Last Supper, Jesus will explain: "This is eternal life: that they know you, the only true God, and the one whom you sent, Jesus Christ" (John

17:3). Jesus comes to reveal us the fatherhood of God. The disciples will be amazed when Jesus will teach to pray: "Our Father," and when they will hear him calling God: Abbá, "my dear Father."

(3) *Exiting the cloud: "He was found alone"*

After the Transfiguration, Christ will be found alone. The voice of the Father will cease and the disciples will remain silent. They exit the cloud and they kept in their heart the voice of the Father: "Listen to him."

Like with some movies, the disciples received a "preview" of Christ's identity and mission. He is not yet victorious. The voice gave them a hint and invited them to walk listening to Jesus.

The disciples receive an indication for their next step: Follow and listen to Jesus. The voice did not tell them all the details of their path. That would be overwhelming. The disciples received light: the light that would lead them to their next stop, their next milestone. God is very respectful and patient with our freedom and our time.

For your prayer

Saint Paul experienced the secret of Jesus. The Son of God came to reveal us the name of God: Our Father. Writing to the Christians in Ephesus he said: "*I kneel before the Father, from whom every family in heaven and on earth is named, that he may grant you in accord with the riches of his glory to be strengthened with power through his Spirit in the inner self, and that Christ may dwell in your hearts through faith*" (Eph 3:14–17).

Monday (Second Week of Lent)

GOSPEL: LK 6:36–38

Jesus said to his disciples: "Be merciful, just as your Father is merciful.

"Stop judging and you will not be judged. Stop condemning and you will not be condemned. Forgive and you will be forgiven. Give and gifts will be given to you; a good measure, packed together, shaken down, and overflowing, will be poured into your lap. For the measure with which you measure will in return be measured out to you."

(1) *Our vocation: become a reflection of God's love*

She was only twenty when she died. In only two decades of life, Maria Teresa Gonzalez-Quevedo got really close to Jesus, through the path of Mary. As a high schooler she wanted to be a reflection of God, following the example of Mary. Around her junior year, when she consecrated herself to Mary, she chose this saying for her medal of consecration: "Mother, let all who look at me see you in me."

We are called to be transfigured, to reflect in our face and our life the glory of God. This transfiguration is the promise of Mount Tabor. The Gospel reminds us today of this high vocation: "Be merciful as your Father is merciful." Saint Matthew offers a similar saying of Jesus: "Be perfect, just as your heavenly Father is perfect" (Mt 5:48). Be perfect; shine as he shines. Do not be satisfied with being a good Catholic. Do not remain in the self-complacency of thinking you are just and nice. Be perfect. Continue growing, since if you do not move forward, you are moving backward.

"Be perfect." But is this not a terrible temptation? Some of us experience the consequences of our perfectionism every day. We think everything must be perfect, even the minuscule detail, and that everything depends on us. As a result, we lose the general vision, the big picture. But Jesus is not calling us to perfectionism, but to be perfect as our Father is perfect, that is, according to Luke, perfect in mercy. God's perfection—what we are called to imitate—is not just power, intelligence: activity, activity, and activity... God is merciful because he is not judging, that is, he is not condemning us, but he always offers his forgiveness.

O Lord, thank you for your great mercy (see Psalm 107:1). You have seen my misery and have heard my prayer. You know my sufferings and you come to save me (see Ex 3:7). Help me to be perfect in mercy. "Let all who look at me see you in me."

(2) *Transfiguring my relationships: a new measure*

Like Jesus on Mount Tabor, we are called to be a reflection of God's mercy. This transformation is our vocation, since we have been created as an image of God and he is merciful. When we offer forgiveness we introduce a new measure of love, overflowing and generous, into our relationships.

Our vocation to be Christ's image comes through the transfiguration of our relationships. Perhaps we are stuck in our marriage, in our relationship with our in-laws, or with our grown children and we think there is nothing new in them. Jesus wants to help us to build these relationships. Faith is a light capable of illuminating all our relationships! (see Pope Francis, *Lumen fidei,* 51, 54). How is this going to happen? God reminds us of the origin and destiny of this "architecture of relationships." The love we give to our parents, spouse, children, in-laws...comes from God, the Creator, and guides us toward him.

Stop judging. Stop condemning. Of course, this is easy to say and difficult to live. But this restraint is the only way to regenerate a relationship and it is the only useful path. What's the sense of judging and condemning? What's its advantage? No fruit comes from judging the others, not even a small one, just bitterness and resentment. You may say: "But my judgment is true!" Of course it is, but is it useful? And on the other hand is not God's gaze of hope over this person more true? Enter into this new measure of God's love and God's hope for this relationship!

(3) *Transfiguration through our humility*

Today's first reading shows us that our transfiguration comes through humility. The prophet Daniel offers us a great prayer you can read and consider. I know we are not worthy, but I know who you are. We are shamefaced …but your face is full of glory, of the glory of forgiveness and mercy. You keep your merciful covenant toward us. Yours, O Lord our God, are compassion and forgiveness (see Dn 9:4–10).

The new measure of divine love implies great humility. When we judge (and condemn), we assume the place of God. We complain about this person or this event, and finally we complain about the Creator of this person and the one who has allowed this event to happen. Whenever I judge, I am judging God. Forgiveness implies that I understand I am not the judge of the world, but a sinner, forgiven by the Lord. I am not called to judge, condemn, and complain, but to receive God's forgiveness and pray for my beloved.

If you judge and condemn your husband or your wife, come to confession this week and receive God's compassion and forgiveness. Offer to your spouse a new measure of love and you will discover the transforming power of Christ's forgiveness in you. This new measure of love and forgiveness is what Mary, the Mother of Jesus, did at the foot of the Cross. You can ask her: "Mother, let all who look at me see you in me."

For your prayer

When you begin your prayer, you may add a new step after the act of presence of God. Saint Ignatius of Loyola invites us to begin our daily prayer with a "preparatory prayer," asking for purity of intention.

You can say something like this with your own words: "*Give light and strength to my heart, O Lord, so that all my intentions, actions, and operations may be directed purely to your service and praise.*"

Tuesday (Second Week of Lent)

GOSPEL: MT 23:1–12

Jesus spoke to the crowds and to his disciples, saying, "The scribes and the Pharisees have taken their seat on the chair of Moses. Therefore, do and observe all things whatsoever they tell you, but do not follow their example. For they preach but they do not practice. They tie up heavy burdens hard to carry and lay them on people's shoulders, but they will not lift a finger to move them. All their works are performed to be seen. They widen their phylacteries and lengthen their tassels. They love places of honor at banquets, seats of honor in synagogues, greetings in marketplaces, and the salutation 'Rabbi.' As for you, do not be called 'Rabbi.' You have but one teacher, and you are all brothers. Call no one on earth your father; you have but one Father in heaven. Do not be called 'Master'; you have but one master, the Christ. The greatest among you must be your servant. Whoever exalts himself will be humbled; but whoever humbles himself will be exalted."

(1) *A hidden transfiguration: preaching and practicing*

The Picture of Dorian Gray (1890) seems to be the only published novel written by Oscar Wilde. Dorian is a young, handsome, and proud man who becomes the subject of a painting. The picture is so beautiful that Dorian, realizing that one day all this beauty will pass away, expresses an evil desire: "I would rather sell my soul if I could ensure that this portrait would age rather than me." The desire will be fulfilled and Dorian will remain years and years in his beauty. The portrait, hidden in his house, will change day by day, not only aging, but also reflecting the proud and evil actions of Dorian.

Our own actions shape our heart and even transform our face. Contrary to Dorian's degeneration, we are being slowly transfigured into Jesus, with the grace of the Holy Spirit. The goodness of our actions, the sacrifice of sleeping a few hours because of our kids, the wrinkles of our worries with our family life...all these actions give shape to our heart and usually also to our face. Not only words, but actions transfigure our life.

Speaking about the scribes and Pharisees, Jesus insists on this divergence: they preach but they do not practice. It is good that they preach, but they should show in their actions what they teach. Our daily life is calling us to this unity between words and actions in our life. Actions, not just words, are necessary.

Jesus does not want the Pharisees to stop preaching, but rather to practice what their speech proclaims. Let us try to better understand the power of our words. As the Pharisees, we speak but we do not live according to these words. Our word—as father, mother, teacher, catechist, priest—will be only really fruitful if it goes together with the example of our actions. But sometimes in our poverty as parents, teachers, priests...we have to say something to our children, students...something we are not yet living. Or better: we have to correct something (don't waste time with this; don't say these words), which is at the same time, our struggle. Our mission (our obligation to say these things to our children) is helping us to be humble and to change. That which we have to say will help us to integrate our actions and our words, to unify our mouth and our hands with our heart.

(2) *Calling to conversion: one who loves you will correct you*

Today Jesus is hard with the scribes and Pharisees. They are not perfect as our Father is perfect because they are not merciful. Really they are merciful with themselves but not with the people. "They tie up heavy burdens hard to carry and lay them on people's shoulders, but they will not lift a finger to move them." They are shepherds—parents, teachers, priests...—who do not take care of their sheep, but they just make profit of it.

"Do not follow their example. For they preach but they do not practice." Let us understand well these words, which are Jesus' s greatest act of mercy toward the Pharisees. Out of love, Christ is calling them to conversion, to change their heart. He is offering them a new path. Even for them there is hope. Some, like Nicodemus and others, will accept the proposal with humility.

> Come now, let us set things right. / ... Though your sins be like scarlet, / they may become white as snow; / Though they be red like crimson, / they may become white as wool" (Is 1:18).

To be merciful as our Father is merciful implies, sometimes, strong words. Of course, we cannot apply this as a general rule. Jesus was meek and humble. Only in special moments, he spoke with these harsh words and tried to awaken the hardened hearts.

(3) *Works are performed to be seen!*

What is the main mistake of the Pharisees? They are preaching, praying, fasting...but all their works are performed to be seen! Our natural question is: To be seen by whom? Fame and honor are powerful idols in our human heart. What are they going to think if I do this? What will they say if...?

Do not imitate the Pharisees, because they do not live under our Father's gaze, but out of vanity. We began our time of Lent under the eyes of the Father and we are called to grow in this tender presence. His eyes are transforming us from ash to a new creature. This re-creation is the transfiguration promised on Mount Tabor: "Whoever exalts himself will be humbled, but whoever humbles himself will be exalted."

For your prayer

Today I propose a challenge for you. Pray the Litany of Humility of Cardinal Merry del Val. Praying them, you will assume great risks: you will ask to be forgotten, to not be consulted… Look at Christ and ask for the gift of humility. You can repeat this litany during this week.

O Jesus! meek and humble of heart, *hear me.*
From the desire of being esteemed, *deliver me, Jesus.*
From the desire of being loved…
From the desire of being extolled…
From the desire of being honored…
From the desire of being praised…
From the desire of being preferred to others…
From the desire of being consulted…
From the desire of being approved…
From the fear of being humiliated…
From the fear of being despised…
From the fear of suffering rebukes…
From the fear of being calumniated…
From the fear of being forgotten …
From the fear of being ridiculed …
From the fear of being wronged …
From the fear of being suspected …
That others may be loved more than I, *Jesus, grant me the grace to desire it.*
That others may be esteemed more than I…
That, in the opinion of the world…
others may increase and I may decrease…
That others may be chosen and I set aside…

That others may be praised and I unnoticed ...
That others may be preferred to me in everything...
That others may become holier than I, provided that I may become as holy as I should...

Wednesday (Second Week of Lent)

GOSPEL: MT 20:17–28

As Jesus was going up to Jerusalem, he took the Twelve disciples aside by themselves, and said to them on the way, "Behold, we are going up to Jerusalem, and the Son of Man will be handed over to the chief priests and the scribes, and they will condemn him to death, and hand him over to the Gentiles to be mocked and scourged and crucified, and he will be raised on the third day." Then the mother of the sons of Zebedee approached Jesus with her sons and did him homage, wishing to ask him for something. He said to her, "What do you wish?" She answered him, "Command that these two sons of mine sit, one at your right and the other at your left, in your kingdom." Jesus said in reply, "You do not know what you are asking. Can you drink the chalice that I am going to drink?" They said to him, "We can." He replied, "My chalice you will indeed drink, but to sit at my right and at my left, this is not mine to give but is for those for whom it has been prepared by my Father." When the ten heard this, they became indignant at the two brothers. But Jesus summoned them and said, "You know that the rulers of the Gentiles lord it over them, and the great ones make their authority over them felt. But it shall not be so among you. Rather, whoever wishes to be great among you shall be your servant; whoever wishes to be first among you shall be your slave. Just so, the Son of Man did not come to be served but to serve and to give his life as a ransom for many."

(1) *Purifying our desires: making them bigger*

We know well the power of a mother. When she asks something for her children she will be insistent and perseverant. Today we contemplate a mother interceding for her children. Her name was very probably Salome (Mk 15:40; Mat 27:56) and she was Zebedee's wife, the mother of James and John. Later she will be present at the foot of the cross and she will go to Jesus' tomb to anoint his body with spices (Mk 16:1).

Salome comes with her two sons, who are, together with Peter, the closest disciples of Jesus. She comes with a request for the Master. Jesus, willing to hear the desires of a loving mother for her children, will ask her: "What do you wish?" A mother has always great desires and expectations for her children. She wants her sons to sit together with Jesus in his kingdom.

Our first thought would be that Salome has too great expectations regarding her children. She asked too much. Jesus should correct her and invite John and James to be humble. But our Lord will answer in a very special way. He will correct Salome because she does not know what she is asking and she will answer with a question: "Can you drink my chalice?." And the brothers will answer: "We can." Jesus surprises us in this dialogue because he doesn't correct this family. He confirms their answer: "Yes, you can, you will drink my chalice." Only at the end he will warn all the disciples against their pride and their desire for power.

The problem of Salome's request is not that she asked to much. Jesus wants us to aim high, to have great expectations for our life. Mediocrity does not belong to the Christian vocabulary. Whenever Jesus enters into our life, he brings greatness of heart, desire of holiness and perfection in our love.

Salome does not know the meaning of her request. She wants worldly honors, prestige and possession for her children. And that is too little for John and James, the disciples of Jesus. They are called to do greater things. That's what Jesus his seventy-two disciples when they came back from their mission: "Behold, I have given you the power 'to tread upon serpents' and scorpions and upon the full force of the enemy and nothing will harm you. Nevertheless, do not rejoice because the spirits are subject to you, but rejoice because your names are written in heaven" (Lk 10:18–20)

We can think that Jesus is asking Salome to reconsider her petition: Aim higher. Your children were created and called by me to do greater things. Ask me that their names may be written in heaven. Ask me that they may become beacons of salvation for the world.

If you are mother or father, grandmother or grandfather, ask Jesus greater things for your children and grandchildren. Do not think small. Pride always aims too low.

(2) *Transfiguration without sacrifice*

The petition of Salome is surrounded by the words of Jesus regarding his passion. He prepares his disciples for his suffering, when he will go up to Jerusalem. There he will be: handed over, condemned, mocked, scourged, crucified...but finally raised and victorious forever.

We can detect here another problem in Salome's petition. She wants her children to be with Christ without being Christ like. She asks for transfiguration without sacrifice, for resurrection without passion. She wants them to follow Jesus but she doesn't want the cross for them.

Suffering belong to our path of growth and education. We usually say "no pain, no gain." Many times we reject the cross for us and for our family and we try to live our friendship with Jesus without moving out of our "comfort zone." In this way, Jesus becomes just a "nice guy" but he is unable to help us to grow and face new challenges in our life. We have sugarcoated him.

In his message for Lent on 2015, Pope Francis has warned us against the dangers of the "globalization of indifference." In this time we are called to be transfigured following Jesus wherever he goes, accepting joys and sufferings with him.

(3) *We can*

Possumus! We can! James and John answered with great courage and maybe also with some kind of unawareness. "We can drink the chalice of Jesus, we can be baptized with his baptism." These two brothers were called "Boanerges," that is, the "sons of thunder." We can imagine they had an interesting temper and probably some anger-related issues. For sure, they were not flematic people.

As we have seen, Jesus confirms their answer. Yes! They will drink his chalice, they will offer their lives for Jesus. We know James will be killed by the sword, early in the 40s, by King Herod Agrippa, the grandson of Herod the Great (Acts 12:1–2). According to a solid tradition, after the Resurrection he proclaimed the Gospel through the Mediterranean Sea and he reached even Spain. For that reason, after his death, some of his disciples will bring his body to the place where he preached the resurrection of Jesus. The humble fisherman of Galilee will be buried at the end of the world, where the sun sets.

We can. Jesus wants us to realize that *with him* we are able to grow and work wonders. "With me, you can." Without me, you can do nothing at all (see John 15:5). This was Benedict XVI's conviction when he was elected pope: "After the great Pope John Paul II, the Cardinals have elected me, a simple and humble labourer in the vineyard of the Lord. The fact that the Lord knows how to work and to act even with inadequate instruments comforts me, and above all I entrust myself to your prayers. Let us move forward in the joy of the Risen Lord, confident of his unfailing help" (April 19, 2005)

For your prayer

According to some scholars, Salome, the mother of James and John, could be Mary's sister (John 19:25).

Today I invite you to pray the *Magnificat* with Saint Mary, Salome, James and John.

Thursday (Second Week of Lent)

GOSPEL: LK 16:19–31

Jesus said to the Pharisees: "There was a rich man who dressed in purple garments and fine linen and dined sumptuously each day. And lying at his door was a poor man named Lazarus, covered with sores, who would gladly have eaten his fill of the scraps that fell from the rich man's table. Dogs even used to come and lick his sores. When the poor man died, he was carried away by angels to the bosom of Abraham. The rich man also died and was buried, and from the netherworld, where he was in torment, he raised his eyes and saw Abraham far off and Lazarus at his side. And he cried out, 'Father Abraham, have pity on me. Send Lazarus to dip the tip of his finger in water and cool my tongue, for I am suffering torment in these flames.' Abraham replied, 'My child, remember that you received what was good during your lifetime while Lazarus likewise received what was bad; but now he is comforted here, whereas you are tormented. Moreover, between us and you a great chasm is established to prevent anyone from crossing who might wish to go from our side to yours or from your side to ours.' He said, 'Then I beg you, father, send him to my father's house, for I have five brothers, so that he may warn them, lest they too come to this place of torment.' But Abraham replied, 'They have Moses and the prophets. Let them listen to them.' He said, 'Oh no, father Abraham, but if someone from the dead goes to them, they will repent.' Then Abraham said, 'If they will not listen to Moses and the prophets, neither will they be persuaded if someone should rise from the dead.'"

(1) *A blind, insensible, deaf rich man*

Jesus addressed this parable to the Pharisees. This rich man dressed in purple garments and fine linen and dined sumptuously each day. We heard a few days ago that the Pharisees widen their phylacteries, lengthen their tassels, and they love places of honor at banquets (see Mt 23:1–12). They are full of themselves. Jesus is again calling them to convert themselves, to open their hearts, and leave space for the action of the Holy Spirit.

This time conversion implies charity, attention to the needy. Even if the rich man belongs to a large family of six brothers, he has not learned to be generous and to offer his richness to the poor. He is completely blind! The poor Lazarus is lying at his door and even the dogs are able to see Lazarus and lick his sores. But this rich man is blind. He is not a "bad person," an evil doer, a thief, a troublemaker, a liar... Just he spends his days dining sumptuously, dressing in purple garments...indifferent to the needs of his brother.

Without faith we are blind. Without the presence of God, we live just for ourselves, we become selfish and lack humanity. Living only for this world, our eyes are unable to see reality as it is; we avoid suffering and those who suffer... Lazarus has been erased from our world.

Without faith, this rich man is also deaf, indifferent to the cries of the poor. He has no eyes to see, no ears to hear. He is just blind, deaf, mute... His life is full of comfort, pleasures, and idols, but he has a great emptiness in his heart. We know the poor is called Lazarus, but the rich man is nameless. Jesus does not give him a name because his life lacks of compassion and love, and therefore it also lacks identity.

Our faith, our encounter with Christ, gives us new eyes, ears, mouth, hands, feet... Christ reveals man to himself! When we look at him we understand the meaning of the human heart. At the sight of the crowds, at the sight of us, Jesus is moved with pity (see Mt 9:36). "Give me, Lord, this compassionate 'gaze,' give me a heart like yours!"

(2) *Transfiguration: the heaven on earth*

We know the end of this "poor rich man." He is in the netherworld, in torment. He received what was good during his lifetime while Lazarus received what was bad. So after a pleasant and rich life he comes to hell. We may think that the rich man began with "heaven" and finished with hell, whereas Lazarus began with suffering and finished with joy in heaven.

But Jesus wants to tell us something else. The rich man is now in torment, but his previous life was not one of a happy man. He was full of pleasures but he was not really living a transfigured existence. For that reason as we have seen, he had no name. During his life he has not built any relationship, any friendship. Jesus does not speak about his family, his wife or children; he has no identity, he is not a son, a spouse, or a father. Only later we know that he has several brothers, but it seems that they live, like him, with no charity; they do not take care of their personal relationships. We can realize that for the rich man, the torment began already on earth. Likewise, heaven begins already in our life, in our relationships. In the joys of our family, we can have a foretaste of our future resurrection.

(3) *The mystery of the mediation: poor signs*

"If they will not listen to Moses and the prophets, neither will they be persuaded if someone should rise from the dead." A last point of this parable is the mystery of mediation. The words of Abraham to the rich man are also the words of Jesus to the Pharisees. We can imagine that the Master is telling them: "If you do not listen to Moses and the prophets, you will not believe even after my resurrection." We know that John, James, and Peter could recall the testimony of Moses and the prophet Elijah on Mount Tabor when they proclaimed Jesus as the Messiah.

The rich man asks for extraordinary revelations or great miracles. He will only receive poor signs: the presence of Lazarus at his door, the humility of Moses and the prophets.

Be humble. Look at the signs the Lord is giving you now in your life. Look at those who are lying at your door: first of all, look at your spouse and children, your parents and siblings, but also the lonely, the poor, and the needy.

For your prayer

Read 1 Cor 13. In my family we used to read this text frequently. My father would ask us to read it and repeat it until we learned it by heart. Keep these words of God in your heart so that you may receive the new eyes, ears, mouth, hands and feet of charity.

Friday (Second Week of Lent)

GOSPEL: MT 21:33–43,45–46

Jesus said to the chief priests and the elders of the people: "Hear another parable. There was a landowner who planted a vineyard, put a hedge around it, dug a wine press in it, and built a tower. Then he leased it to tenants and went on a journey. When vintage time drew near, he sent his servants to the tenants to obtain his produce. But the tenants seized the servants and one they beat, another they killed, and a third they stoned. Again he sent other servants, more numerous than the first ones, but they treated them in the same way. Finally, he sent his son to them, thinking, 'They will respect my son.' But when the tenants saw the son, they said to one another, 'This is the heir. Come, let us kill him and acquire his inheritance.' They seized him, threw him out of the vineyard, and killed him. What will the owner of the vineyard do to those tenants when he comes?" They answered him, "He will put those wretched men to a wretched death and lease his vineyard to other tenants who will give him the produce at the proper times." Jesus said to them, "Did you never read in the Scriptures: / The stone that the builders rejected / has become the cornerstone; / by the Lord has this been done, / and it is wonderful in our eyes? Therefore, I say to you, the Kingdom of God will be taken away from you and given to a people that will produce its fruit." When the chief priests and the Pharisees heard his parables, they knew that he was speaking about them. And although they were attempting to arrest him, they feared the crowds, for they regarded him as a prophet.

(1) *Transfiguration: an impossible mission?*

During these days we are reflecting on Jesus' and our transfiguration. But is that possible? You may ask me: Do you read the newspapers? Do you speak with your neighbors? Don't you see the sins of the world? Evil is everywhere. The wicked triumph and the weak are destroyed. Transfiguration? This is simply impossible, just a consolation for the poor.

Consider even today's first reading, the story of Joseph. The chosen brother, the most beloved son is almost murdered by his siblings and finally "just" sold as a slave to the Ishmaelites. The brothers against their brother. And this was not an isolated case: think about Cain and Abel, Isaac and Ismael, Esau and Jacob... The whole story of Israel is about families suffering and struggling.

But let us consider the whole story. What happens after Joseph is sold? After several adventures, we find Joseph very close to the King of Egypt and prepared to welcome his family when famine comes. And we see Jacob's family in need, coming to Egypt, where Joseph saves them from starving.

Transfiguration comes sometimes through mysterious designs. This mystery is what Psalm 105 invites us to understand: Remember the marvels the Lord has done. Of course, God does not want the sin of the brothers, but even this envy is used by him to grant the family a greater blessing. Remember the marvels of the Lord:

> He called down a famine on the land / ... He had sent a man ahead of them, / Joseph, sold as a slave. / They shackled his feet with chains; / collared his neck in iron / ... [The king] made him lord over his household, / ruler over all his possessions (Ps 105:16, 17–18, 21).

Be patient, stay faithful to your vocation and you will understand. For "[w]e know that all things work for good of those who love God, who are called according to his purpose" (Rom 8:28).

(2) *The greatest love of Jesus*

In today's Gospel, Jesus tells us a parable, which reminds us of the life of Joseph. A landowner plants a vineyard and takes care of it, building a tower, digging a wine press, and putting a hedge around it. And then he leases it to tenants and goes on a journey. Like Jacob sent his son Joseph to see his brothers, the landowner sends many servants to obtain his produce and finally he sends his son. Jacob's children, thanks to the intercession of Reuben and Judah, did not kill Joseph, but sold him as a slave. But the tenants of the vineyard do kill the son.

Jesus is speaking about himself, sent by the Father. He addresses his parable to the chief priests and the elders of the people, so that they may remember the stories of the Patriarchs which are fulfilled in him. And they understand his message but do not follow his invitation to conversion and faith.

Death is spared to Joseph but not to Jesus. The Transfiguration comes also here. Joseph, rejected and sold by his siblings, becomes the savior of the family. Jesus, not only rejected by the elders and chief priests and sold by his disciple Judas, but also persecuted and crucified, overcomes death. The stone rejected by the builders becomes the cornerstone!

In my childhood memories, when my priestly vocation was maturing, I keep some visits to the beautiful Church of Saint Francis of

Borja in Madrid. Entering the temple from the noise of downtown (right in front of the US Embassy), I would find a dwelling of silence and adoration. In the tabernacle the presence of Jesus was manifested with some words, perhaps the first latin I learned: Nolite timere. Ego vicit mundum! "Do not be afraid. I have won over the world." Mine is the victory! After a few minutes of prayer, I would go out again into the busy city, but with new eyes, transfigured by the presence of Jesus Christ, the Savior.

(3) *Transfiguration through forgiveness*

Jesus finishes his parable with an interesting question: What will the owner of the vineyard do to those tenants when he comes? According to the people, the landowner should kill those wretched men and lease his vineyard to other tenants. Jesus does not comment on their answer. He just advises them: if you do not convert to God, the kingdom will be taken away from you and given to a people that will produce its fruit. But what about the wretched death to these wretched men? With his own life, Jesus offers us an answer. He, the just man, the Son of God, suffers a wretched death. And from the Cross, Jesus does not ask his Father to send those men to a wretched death. Rather he repeats unceasingly: "Father, forgive them, they know not what they do" (Lk 23:34).

☙ *For your prayer*

Today you can pray with the eighth chapter of the Letter of Saint Paul to the Romans (especially, Rom 8:26–32). Ask the Lord to help you to understand his project of holiness for your family.

The Spirit too comes to the aid of our weakness; for we do not know how to pray as we ought, but the Spirit itself intercedes with inexpressible groanings. And the one who searches hearts knows what is the intention of the Spirit, because it intercedes for the holy ones according to God's will.

We know that all things work for good for those who love God, who are called according to his purpose...

What then shall we say to this? If God is for us, who can be against us? He who did not spare his own Son but handed him over for us all, how will he not also give us everything else along with him? (Rom 8:26–32).

Saturday (Second Week of Lent)

GOSPEL: LK 15:1–3, 11–32

Tax collectors and sinners were all drawing near to listen to [Jesus], but the Pharisees and scribes began to complain, saying, "This man welcomes sinners and eats with them." So to them he addressed this parable. "A man had two sons, and the younger son said to his father, 'Father, give me the share of your estate that should come to me.' So the father divided the property between them. After a few days, the younger son collected all his belongings and set off to a distant country where he squandered his inheritance on a life of dissipation. When he had freely spent everything, a severe famine struck that country, and he found himself in dire need. So he hired himself out to one of the local citizens who sent him to his farm to tend the swine. And he longed to eat his fill of the pods on which the swine fed, but nobody gave him any. Coming to his senses he thought, 'How many of my father's hired workers have more than enough food to eat, but here am I, dying from hunger. I shall get up and go to my father and I shall say to him, "Father, I have sinned against heaven and against you. I no longer deserve to be called your son; treat me as you would treat one of your hired workers."' So he got up and went back to his father. While he was still a long way off, his father caught sight of him, and was filled with compassion. He ran to his son, embraced him and kissed him. His son said to him, 'Father, I have sinned against heaven and against you; I no longer deserve to be called your son.' But his father ordered his servants, 'Quickly, bring the finest robe and put it on him; put a ring on his finger and sandals on his feet. Take the fattened calf and slaughter it. Then let us celebrate with a feast, because this son of mine was dead, and has come to life again; he was lost, and has been found.' Then the celebration began. Now the older son had been out in the field and, on his way back, as he neared the house, he heard the sound of music and dancing. He called one of the servants and asked what this might mean. The servant said to him, 'Your brother has returned and your father has slaughtered the fattened calf because he has him back safe and sound.' He became angry, and when he refused to enter the house, his father came out and pleaded with him. He said to his father in reply, 'Look, all these years I served you and not once did I disobey your orders; yet you never gave me even a young goat to feast on with my friends. But when your son returns who swallowed up your property with prostitutes, for him you slaughter the fattened calf.' He said to him, 'My son, you are here with me always; everything I have is yours. But now we must celebrate and rejoice, because your brother was dead and has come to life again; he was lost and has been found.'"

Today we hear another parable related to a family. This time the main problem is not only the bad relationship between the brothers, but especially the connection between the father and his two children.

(1) *The "prodigal Father"*

We usually consider this parable as the one of the "prodigal son." But, according to Jesus, who is the main character of the story? We know why he tells this parable. The Pharisees and scribes are complaining because Jesus is welcoming sinners and eating with them. The Master wants to introduce them—and us—into the mystery of God. Who is our Creator?

The real topic of this parable is not the prodigal son, nor the proud older son, but the "prodigal father." He is not prodigal because a great spender, but prodigal because he is always generous, abundant in his mercy. Jesus reveals to us that God is the perseverant and generous Father. The landowner of the vineyard in yesterday's Gospel is not only the Father of Jesus Christ, but also ours. Whether we are far away or living and working in his house, he is always waiting for our return. His desire is this: the transfiguration of our relationships, our reconciliation with him, and thus reconciliation within our family.

(2) *Who is further from the Father?*

The younger son decides to abandon his house, the house of his father. Long before, he had already desired to do so. Finally he inflicts this great pain on his father. When he asks for the share of his estate, this young man is "killing" his father. We cannot imagine the great grief in the father's heart. The son is asking for what he should receive after his father's death: "For me, you are no more living. I do not want your presence, but only my belongings." And of course, together with the father, he ignores and abandons (he "kills") his brother.

His next step is to squander his inheritance on a life of dissipation and finally, as a result, to tend the swine. He even arrives to longing to eat his fill of the pods on which the swine feed, but nobody gives him any. It could not be worse for him. We can remember also the spiritual meaning of the pigs. They were impure animals that a good Jew should not eat nor touch.

In this great desolation, the younger son keeps a treasure in his heart: the memory of the father. In the middle of all this frustration and turmoil, he conserves this name: "Father, I have sinned against heaven and against you." In his desire—first of all just of bread—the voice of the Father is resounding in his heart: "Come to me, all you who labor and are burdened, and I will give you rest" (Mt 11:28). In the worst moments of your desolation, anger, and grief, remember who is God. He is always welcoming because his name is "Father"!

(3) *The older son: who is further from the Father?*

Let us think also about the older brother. This parable is addressed to the Pharisees and scribes, who complain about Jesus' mercy: Why are you welcoming and eating with these sinners?

The older son is very far from the father. He is living at his home and working for him, but his heart is not united with his father; his desires, joys, and sufferings are not the same. We do not find the word "Father" on his lips, because he has been living as a servant, as a slave at his father's house. "All these years I served you and not once did I disobey your orders." It is not enough to serve and obey. The father wants his son to "resonate" with him, to mourn with him, and to rejoice and celebrate with him. Idem velle, idem nolle. To desire the same things and to reject the same things: that is, the harmony of wills, the concord generated by love.

Why cannot the older son resonate with his father? He has not acknowledged the gift of sonship and the unconditional love it implies. For that reason he trusts in his own works: I have served, I have obeyed... And he misses the great point: "My son, you are here with me always; everything I have is yours." Far from his father, he is unable to share his joy and he does not welcome his younger brother. He calls him "your son," but never "my brother."

The parable finishes open. Now, Jesus seems to say to the Pharisees, it is your turn. You decide. As the older son, you are called to conversion. Enter into the heart of the Father! Expel any judgment and complaint, which make happiness impossible! Perhaps you are faithful to your Sunday Mass and even to your frequent confession, and this is great. But do not think you are better, that you are justified by your actions.

☙ *For your prayer*

Today you can pray with the different characters of this parable. Imagine you are the prodigal son and the older son. Imagine you are the Father and look at your own family.

O Father, I have sinned against heaven and against you, I have been with idols and pleasures far from your presence. I no longer deserve to be called your son.

O Father, I have sinned against heaven and against you, I have been in your house all this time, but I am far from you and from my brothers. I have been angry and resentful against my family, thinking I am clean and holy. I no longer deserve to be called your son.

Pray with Saint Augustine (*Confessions*, 7), a prodigal son:

Late have I loved you, O Beauty ever ancient, ever new. Late have I loved you! You were within me, but I was outside, and it was there that I searched for you. In my unloveliness I plunged into the lovely things which you created. You were with me, but I was not with you. Created things kept me from you; yet if they had not been in you they would not have been at all. You called, you shouted, and you broke through my deafness. You flashed, you shone, and you dispelled my blindness. You breathed your fragrance on me; I drew in breath and now I pant for you. I have tasted you, now I hunger and thirst for more. You touched me, and I burned for your peace.

II

Encountering Christ

WE cannot look at Christ from far away. We have seen him on the mount of the temptations and on the mount of glory. When we see him, he invites us to enter into his life. When we see him, we realize that he has seen us first; he has loved us and calls us to be with him. His desire and our desire go together.

During these next weeks we will make friends. On these three Sundays we will consider the great stories of the Samaritan woman, the blind man, and Lazarus when they encounter Jesus. To encounter Christ is the essence of being Christian. In his first encyclical, Pope Benedict XVI explained to us that Christianity is not just about a deep idea, a great decision, or a wonderful ethic; it is about a personal encounter with Christ, who transforms our lives and reveals a new horizon to our lives (see *Deus Caritas Est,* 1).

These three persons are ash, hopeless flesh without hope: one is thirsty and unsatisfied, another, blind, never having seen the light, and Lazarus is completely dead. They receive the presence of Christ in their lives as a great surprise; Christ is new water for the Samaritan woman, who had been already with five husbands! And she is living with a sixth man who is not her husband. Christ is light for the blind man, after thirty-eight years without colors and brightness. Christ is new life for Lazarus, who has already spent four days dead in the tomb.

Water, light, and life. This encounter is the beginning of a new path in their lives. For us, on our path from ash toward water, these three encounters are a reminder of our baptism. In fact, the first sacrament means "immersion in water" (to baptize); the first Christians called it "the enlightenment" (Photismós). Some fathers of the Church compare the baptismal font with the tomb and the mother's womb, the place of death and new life.

Our thirsty desire, our darkness, and our mortal flesh will find in Christ the Source of water, the Light of the world and the Voice that brings new life. In our Easter Vigil, in the "greatest of all the vigils" we will find this fire in the middle of the night, this water, and this powerful Word of God. These elements are the structure of the vigil in which four signs define four moments: light, water, word, and bread and wine. Through the Easter candle, the sprinkling water, and the readings of the Holy Scripture we will prepare our heart to receive the body and blood of Christ, to share in his passion. Fire, water, word, and bread: these elements will be our path this last part of Lent.

THE SAMARITAN WOMAN: OUR DESIRE

(THIRD WEEK OF LENT)

Third Sunday of Lent (A)

GOSPEL: JN 4:5–42

Jesus came to a town of Samaria called Sychar, near the plot of land that Jacob had given to his son Joseph. Jacob's well was there. Jesus, tired from his journey, sat down there at the well. It was about noon.

A woman of Samaria came to draw water. Jesus said to her, "Give me a drink." His disciples had gone into the town to buy food. The Samaritan woman said to him, "How can you, a Jew, ask me, a Samaritan woman, for a drink?"—For Jews use nothing in common with Samaritans.— Jesus answered and said to her, "If you knew the gift of God and who is saying to you, 'Give me a drink,' you would have asked him and he would have given you living water." The woman said to him, "Sir, you do not even have a bucket and the cistern is deep; where then can you get this living water? Are you greater than our father Jacob, who gave us this cistern and drank from it himself with his children and his flocks?" Jesus answered and said to her, "Everyone who drinks this water will be thirsty again; but whoever drinks the water I shall give will never thirst; the water I shall give will become in him a spring of water welling up to eternal life." The woman said to him, "Sir, give me this water, so that I may not be thirsty or have to keep coming here to draw water."

Jesus said to her, "Go call your husband and come back." The woman answered and said to him, "I do not have a husband." Jesus answered her, "You are right in saying, 'I do not have a husband.' For you have had five husbands, and the one you have now is not your husband. What you have said is true." The woman said to him, "Sir, I can see that you are a prophet. Our ancestors worshiped on this mountain; but you people say that the place to worship is in Jerusalem." Jesus said to her, "Believe me, woman, the hour is coming when you will worship the Father neither on this mountain nor in Jerusalem. You people worship what you do not understand; we worship what we understand, because salvation is from the Jews. But the hour is coming, and is now here, when true worshipers will worship the Father in Spirit and truth; and indeed the Father seeks such people to worship him. God is Spirit, and those who worship him must worship in Spirit and truth." The woman said to him, "I know that the Messiah is coming, the one called the Christ; when he comes, he will tell us everything." Jesus said to her, "I am he, the one speaking with you."

At that moment his disciples returned, and were amazed that he was talking with a woman, but still no one said, "What are you looking for?" or "Why are you talking with her?" The woman left her water jar and went into the town and said to the people, "Come see a man who told me everything I have done. Could he possibly be the Christ?" They went out of the town and came to him. Meanwhile, the disciples urged him, "Rabbi, eat." But he said to them, "I have food to eat of which you do not know." So the disciples said to one another, "Could someone have brought him something to eat?" Jesus said to them, "My food is to do the will of the one who sent me and to finish his work. Do you not say, 'In four months the harvest will be here'? I tell you, look up and see the fields ripe for the harvest. The reaper is already receiving payment and gathering crops for eternal life, so that the sower and reaper can rejoice together. For here the saying is verified that 'One sows and another reaps.' I sent you to reap what you have not worked for; others have done the work, and you are sharing the fruits of their work."

Many of the Samaritans of that town began to believe in him because of the word of the woman who testified, "He told me everything I have done." When the Samaritans came to him, they invited him to stay with them; and he stayed there two days. Many more began to believe in him because of his word, and they said to the woman, "We no longer believe because of your word; for we have heard for ourselves, and we know that this is truly the savior of the world."

(1) *Who are the thirsty?*

The Middle Eastern peoples know well the priceless value of water. The water, the presence of a well or a fountain, is a synonym of life, strength, hope. But at the same time, in these regions it is also frequent to experience the destructive power of water: great torrents, unending rains like that which destroyed the land in times of Noah.

Jesus comes with the disciples to Jacob's well, sits down there, and waits. The place of this first encounter of Jesus is a well: the place where the thirsty, the unsatisfied come. The disciples leave him and he remains there waiting for us.

What is Jesus waiting for? It is about noon. Jesus is tired from his journey. They have been walking under the sun. Jesus is thirsty and needs water, but he has nothing with which to draw it from the well. When the Samaritan arrives, he asks her: "Give me water." But Jesus' thirst reveals to us a deeper desire. He comes to the well—the place of human desire—and waits there. He welcomes the Samaritan and begins a dialogue with her. His thirst reveals something much deeper than the water of this well. Jesus desires the happiness of this woman and he wants to offer his love, his water of new life. Jesus has not come to the well because he is thirsty but because he wants to encounter the thirsty.

What is the Samaritan woman looking for? It is about noon. The Samaritan is tired from her life. She has been looking for happiness and joy without success. It is about noon; it is not time to come to draw water. The women of the village came early in the morning, when it was still cool. Now nobody is there. The Samaritan comes because she does not want to meet the other women with their gossiping against her; she is the sinner, the one who has lived with five husbands... In her despair, coming one day more to the well, she finds Jesus.

Therefore at the well we witness the encounter of two desires. Christ is One who desires me and he is the One I desire in all my desires. In this encounter Jesus takes the lead of the dialogue, he is proactive. "O God, you are my God— / it is you I seek! / For you my body yearns; / for you my soul thirsts, / In a land parched, lifeless, / and without water" (Ps 63:2). "As the deer longs for streams of water, / so my soul longs for you, O God. / My soul thirsts for God, the living God" (Ps 42:2–3).

(2) *The path of the Samaritan*

After this first encounter, the dialogue begins. According to the barrier between Jews and Samaritans, they were called to remain in mutual indifference. Jesus is the one who breaks the icy silence, asking with humility: "Give me water." The Creator of heaven and earth, the origin of life, asks for a drink in order to offer a river of living water.

During the dialogue we discover a progressive double revelation. Who is Jesus? The Samaritan understands she is before a special person. She calls him "Jew," but then "sir," "prophet," and finally she asks the Samaritans of her town: "Come and see a man who told me everything I have done. Could he possibly be the Messiah?" (Jn 4:29). At the same time, Jesus reveals to this woman her own mystery. Who am I? Jesus is the voice that, coming from afar, is able to tell her the truth of her life. He does this without false sweetness and without condemnation, but calling her to conversion. You have had five husbands and the one you have now is not your husband.

This is your truth. Now, come to me. If only you knew the gift of God! Whoever drinks the water I shall give will never thirst. I want to heal and purify the desires of your heart. You have a lot of desires, anxiety, frustration… Come to me. I will not give you the satisfaction of all your desires but I will do something greater; I will enlarge them, transforming them into hope.

(3) *Becoming a disciple*

After her short meeting with Jesus, the Samaritan becomes an apostle and makes new disciples of Jesus. "Come and see this man!" The words of this "Jew-lord-prophet and maybe-Messiah" are accomplished in her. The water she has received becomes in her a spring of water for her neighbors. She cannot remain silent with the joy of having encountered Jesus. "Let anyone who thirsts come to me and drink. Whoever believes in me, as scripture says: / 'Rivers of living water will flow from within him'" (Jn 7:37–38).

The gift you have received is not for yourself. Your faith is like the light of a candle; it wants to illuminate the world and light other candles. A lamp is not brought in to be placed under a bushel basket, under a bed. It is called to be placed on a lamp stand! (see Mk 4:21).

Like the Samaritan woman, we are called to speak about our encounter with Christ. We know we are sinners, like her, but Jesus has given us the gift of his friendship. Do not be afraid. Reach out, first of all, to your spouse and children, then to your parents, siblings, in-laws, to your friends, neighbors, and co-workers. Invite them: "Come and see this man. He has told me everything I have done." Lent is time of mission. Do not be afraid of speaking about Jesus. You will be surprised to find so many Samaritan men and women, thirsty for hearing about God. Become a disciple of the heart of Jesus.

For your prayer

On the cross Jesus cries: "I thirst." Like the Samaritan woman, I can help Jesus and offer him the water of my desire. You can pray today with the beautiful text of Mother Teresa of Calcutta. "I thirst." These words changed her life.

I thirst for you. Yes, that is the only way to even begin to describe my love for you. I thirst for you. I thirst to love you and to be loved by you—that is how precious you are to me. I thirst for you. Come to Me, and I will fill your heart and heal your wounds. I will make you a new creation, and give you peace, even in all your trials I thirst for you. You must never doubt my mercy, my acceptance of you, my desire to forgive, my longing to bless you and live my life in you. I thirst for you. If you feel unimportant in the eyes of the world, that matters not at all. For me, there is no one any more important in the entire world than you. I thirst for you. Open to me, come to me, thirst for me, give me your life—and I will prove to you how important you are to my Heart.

THE PURIFICATION OF THE TEMPLE: OUR DESIRE

(THIRD WEEK OF LENT)

Third Sunday of Lent (B)

GOSPEL: JN 2:13–25

Since the Passover of the Jews was near, Jesus went up to Jerusalem. He found in the temple area those who sold oxen, sheep, and doves, as well as the money changers seated there. He made a whip out of cords and drove them all out of the temple area, with the sheep and oxen, and spilled the coins of the money changers and overturned their tables, and to those who sold doves he said, "Take these out of here, and stop making my Father's house a marketplace." His disciples recalled the words of Scripture, / Zeal for your house will consume me./ At this the Jews answered and said to him, "What sign can you show us for doing this?" Jesus answered and said to them, "Destroy this temple and in three days I will raise it up." The Jews said, "This temple has been under construction for forty-six years, and you will raise it up in three days?" But he was speaking about the temple of his body. Therefore, when he was raised from the dead, his disciples remembered that he had said this, and they came to believe the Scripture and the word Jesus had spoken.

While he was in Jerusalem for the feast of Passover, many began to believe in his name when they saw the signs he was doing. But Jesus would not trust himself to them because he knew them all, and did not need anyone to testify about human nature. He himself understood it well.

(1) *Jesus' Anger Management*

Praying to the Father, Jesus invited us once to learn from him: *Learn from me, because I am meek and and humble of heart* (Mt 11:29). And his life will be, from the beginning to the end, an example of this meekness and humility. Today's gospel, however, shows us an angry Jesus who makes a whip out of cords and drives the money changers of the temple area, spills their coins, and overturns their tables. What happened to Jesus? Why was he so angry?

First of all, we learn today that there are good reasons to be angry. When our family is at risk, when we need a great effort to overcome something evil, we need the passion—not the vice—of anger. Anger is a natural reaction to obstacles or threats. When well educated, it gives us fortitude, strength, perseverance… According to Saint Gregory the Great, our reason will oppose the evil more effectively when anger ministers at her side.

But anger is evil when it becomes blind wrath, revengeful resentment or bitterness of spirit. As the Sacred Scripture says, "fools give vent to all their anger, but the wise, biding their time, control it" (Prov 29:11).

Today Jesus is angry. But even in his anger, he is meek and respects the poor. John gives us this particular of Jesus' purification of the temple. He will treat specially those "who sold doves," those who were serving the poor, and he will not overturn their tables. Those who could not afford an animal of the flock could offered instead two turtledoves or two young pigeons (Lev 5:1–13; 12:2–8). This is what Mary and Joseph, the holy and poor family, did when Jesus was born (Lk 2:7).

But the important question regarding our passions is its origin and destination: Why is Jesus so angry? And what for?

We understand Jesus' anger if we consider the importance of the Temple of Jerusalem. For the Jews, the Temple was the place of God's presence, a place of due pilgrimage, where they would pray and present their offerings. At the heart of the temple is was the *Holy of holies* (Sancta Sanctorum). This room was in total darkness and contained the Ark of the Covenant, in which was placed the Tablets of the Covenant, Aaron's rod and a pot of manna (Heb 9:4). The place was so important that it could be entered only by the High Priest on Yom Kippur (once a year).

For Jesus, the temple is something more than the memorial of the presence and action of God. As he explains to us today, this is "my Father's house": not just a place to remember God's wonders, but a place where we encounter him. We can now understand better Jesus' anger: the house of his beloved Father has been transformed into a marketplace, not a sanctuary of gratitude and adoration, but a place of finances and business. For that reason, zeal for the Father's house consumes Jesus.

Looking at Jesus' anger we can consider our anger and the reasons which make us lose our patience. Many times—most of the times—it is not the zeal for the Father's house what consumes us, but our wounded pride, our selfishness... On the other hand, when we see Jesus reacting with holy anger, we can look at our cowardness, our silences, which are "politically correct," but no Christ-like.

(2) *Forty-six years—three days*

But today we are not just remembering the glory of the temple of Jerusalem. When he was asked about the meaning of his actions, Jesus replied to the Jews with a mysterious and challenging answer: "Destroy this temple and in three days I will raise it up."

The gospel of John is always an invitation to go beyond and understand everything in a deeper way. As many times before, Jesus invites the Jews to follow him in his discussion about the temple.

Jesus knows that the gorgeous temple of Jerusalem was built in forty-six years. And, of course, what took men so many years, God can do it in a few days or hours, or in a second. But now, he is offering the Jews a sign. The temple, his Father's house, the place of God's action, is not any more this enormous building, but his own body, the body of the Son of God. This is the sign Jesus offers them: They will destroy his body and he will rebuild it in three days. The resurrection will be the sign of his authority.

The body of Jesus is the new temple of Jerusalem. In him we find the real and living presence of God, who has come to stay with us, to laugh and cry with us, to eat, drink and fast with us. We don't need any more to go and offer sacrifices in the temple of Jerusalem, because in Christ God has offered to us the gift of his presence.

(3) *We are the temple*

Today's gospel reveals also us our dignity. Christ comes to purify the temple and he reveals himself as the new "Father's house," the new place where we encounter God. His body is the new temple that will be destroyed and rebuilt in three days.

And what about us? Through his death and resurrection, Jesus has purchased us at a price. Our bodies are not any more ourselves but they are temples of the holy Spirit within us, whom we have from God (1 Cor 6:18). As Saint Paul explains to the Corinthians, the body is "for the Lord, and the Lord is for the body; God raised the Lord and will also raise us by his power" (1 Cor 6:13–14).

Therefore, the purification of the temple of Jerusalem invites us to look at our bodies as members of Christ. Let us glorify God in our body! Let us give him thanks for the gift of our body. We can also look at our spouse and children, glorifying God for their bodies, for these small or big temples of the Holy Spirit.

For your prayer

Pray with the words of St. Symeon the New Theologian, a great mystic of the tenth century, speaking about the beauty of our body:

"*O wonder! I am vigilant, I am full of respect for myself, of reverence and of fear, as I would be were I before You; I do not know what to do, I am seized by fear, I do not know where to sit, where to go, where to put these members which are yours; in what deeds, in what works shall I use them, these amazing divine marvels!*" (*Hymns* 2, 19–27).

THE FIG TREE: OUR DESIRE

(THIRD WEEK OF LENT)

Third Sunday of Lent (*C*)

GOSPEL: LK 13: 1–9

At that time some people who were present there told him about the Galileans whose blood Pilate had mingled with the blood of their sacrifices. He said to them in reply, "Do you think that because these Galileans suffered in this way they were greater sinners than all other Galileans? By no means! But I tell you, if you do not repent, you will all perish as they did! Or those eighteen people who were killed when the tower at Siloam fell on them—do you think they were more guilty than everyone else who lived in Jerusalem? By no means! But I tell you, if you do not repent, you will all perish as they did!"

And he told them this parable: "There once was a person who had a fig tree planted in his orchard, and when he came in search of fruit on it but found none, he said to the gardener, 'For three years now I have come in search of fruit on this fig tree but have found none. [So] cut it down. Why should it exhaust the soil?' He said to him in reply, 'Sir, leave it for this year also, and I shall cultivate the ground around it and fertilize it; it may bear fruit in the future. If not you can cut it down.'"

(1) *God's desire: our fruitfulness*

Today's gospel is a strong invitation to conversion. Jesus recalls the news of his days, some tragedies which struck the heart of his listeners. There was a brutal repression in the Temple by the Romans and the tragic death of eighteen people, killed when the tower in Siloam collapsed. Then he addressed a question to the people: do you think they were more guilty than us? By no means!

The judgment of the people was that those who died in such circumstances were sinners and they were punished by God. Therefore they believed they were upright and safe from such accidents.

Jesus does not recall these events so that we may be afraid. He wants to help us read these tragedies as a call to conversion, to change our lives. I am not better nor worse than those who died when the towers in New York collapsed. Probably I am less courageous than the firemen who gave their lives helping there. Life has been given to me as a gift.

The call to conversion is the call to fruitfulness. God wants our lives to be fruitful. Jesus compares our existence with the life of a fig-tree. During three years, the Lord has come to us and he has found no fruit. He is sad and he thinks it may be better to cut it down.

Saint Augustine explains this parable comparing the fig-tree with the human race. In the three years without fruit, he sees the three times of our history: one before the law, the second under the law, the third under grace. After the fall, Adam and Eve clothed themselves with fig-leaves. In the Gospel we will see Jesus cursing a fig tree for not producing fruit—a sign of the sinful nation of Israel.

We are like a fig-tree, called to offer sweet fruits, but right now empty. Christ comes in search of fruit because he wants our happiness, he wants for us a life fully alive.

(2) *The intercession: Sir, be patient with him*

In the parable of Jesus we can distinguish two different persons taking care of the orchard. One is the one who planted the fig-tree, our Creator, the other is the gardener, who will intercede for the tree, asking for more time. "Sir, leave it for this year also, and I shall cultivate the ground around it and fertilize it..."

This dialogue between the gardener and the one who planted the tree is the dialogue of the Passion of the Lord, the dialogue we witness at every Mass. Christ, our redeemer, our gardener, speaks to the Father and intercedes for us. "Sir, be patient with him!" As Saint Augustine beautifully puts it, "the merciful intercedes before the merciful" (*Sermo* 254, 3). In every Eucharist, we offer the sacrifice of Jesus Christ to God the Father: Through Him and with Him and in Him...

Christ, the gardener, has given us the mission of cultivating an orchard. As parents or grandparents, but also as siblings, uncles and aunts...we are called to take care of the garden of our family. God needs us to intercede before him for our relatives and friends: "Sir, be patient with my child, I shall cultivate the ground around it and fertilize it. Sir, be patient with my spouse..."

(3) *God gives me time*

Jesus has come so that we may bear fruit and bear it abundantly (John 10:10). He will do whatever is necessary to accomplish his mission (always respecting our freedom). Christ is willing to everything, his time, his reputation, his body and blood...so that we may be fruitful and joyful.

The time of our lives is a gift that comes from the generosity of Jesus. He is praying for us before the Father so that we may be fruitful. Each second, each minute of our life comes from his love, from his offering in the Cross.

Thanks to Jesus, we have time to grow, flourish and fructify. God gives me more time! This fact is not supposed to generate anxiety in us, but just the contrary, great peace. This time is time of grace. It is time I should not waste with internet, facebook, videogames, empty distractions... It is time I am called to give to my beloved, to my Lord, to my family.

During this time of God's patience, we know that Jesus, the gardener, is at work. Through his Holy Spirit, he will cultivate the ground around us and fertilize us, he will prune us, he will contemplate our shoot with hope and our fruits with joy.

For your prayer

Every morning, receive the new day as a gift from the hands of Christ, the gardener.

Thank you, Jesus, for these twenty-four new hours, thank you for your work of gardener in me, in my spouse, children, friends...

Monday (Third Week of Lent)

GOSPEL: LK 4:24–30

Jesus said to the people in the synagogue at Nazareth: "Amen, I say to you, no prophet is accepted in his own native place. Indeed, I tell you, there were many widows in Israel in the days of Elijah when the sky was closed for three and a half years and a severe famine spread over the entire land. It was to none of these that Elijah was sent, but only to a widow in Zarephath in the land of Sidon. Again, there were many lepers in Israel during the time of Elisha the prophet; yet not one of them was cleansed, but only Naaman the Syrian." When the people in the synagogue heard this, they were all filled with fury. They rose up, drove him out of the town, and led him to the brow of the hill on which their town had been built, to hurl him down headlong. But he passed through the midst of them and went away.

(1) *Small desires, small hope*

Jesus comes to Nazareth but he makes no miracles there. He works no wonders because he finds no faith. He finds no desire for him. As to Jacob's well, he comes thirsty to Nazareth with the great desire of offering his love. But he can not make any miracle. In his compatriots he discovers the lack of desire. The people there are already judging him and considering him unnecessary in their lives. "We know who you are, we know where do you come from. We do not need you. We are ok without you."

This Gospel shows us one of the false ways of answering to the restlessness of our desire. The temptation consists in the satisfaction of our small desires. "Be satisfied with your life. Do not desire things that surpass your power, like happiness or holiness. Just enjoy and live a comfortable life."

It is a sad day for Jesus. The people of Nazareth are closed to his word and to his stream of living water. They want to satisfy their daily thirst and nothing else. And like the prodigal son feeding the pigs, like the older son in his life of abiding by the law, like the young rich man coming back to his possessions, they are living without hope.

(2) *Great hope through small details*

The word of God offers us another answer to the mystery of our restlessness. Naaman, the Syrian leper strongly desires to be healed.

His illness moves him toward Elisha, the powerful prophet. When Naaman arrives after a long trip, Elisha sends him a message asking him to wash seven times in the Jordan. This direction is the test of obedience.

Naaman becomes upset. He had thought the prophet would come out and would stand before him invoking the Lord his God and would cure the leprosy. But instead of doing this, Elisha just asks him to wash himself in a small and unknown river. This command is the great scandal. Naaman wants to be healed but he does not accept the poverty of this act of obedience.

Jesus asks from us small details. Do you really want to be healed? Then, why do you set the limits and conditions? If he had asked you to give something really demanding in order to save your life, would you not have done it? (see 2 Kgs 5:13). All the more now, since he says to you, "forgive your spouse for this moment of anger, do not gossip any more about your mother-in-law, go and wash your sins every month in confession," should you do as he says. A great gift comes through small details.

(3) *Whatever you ask me*

Naaman is saved through his friends and servants. When he is about to leave the place full of fury, a servant invites him to be humble and obey. We may think his servants risked their lives in order to save him. But this time Naaman is humble enough to accept the counsel. He washes in the Jordan seven times and he is clean.

"Do whatever he tells you" (Jn 2:5). We need good friends—our children also need them—that may tell us the truth of our lives. "Do whatever he tells you!" In Mary we find a special friend and counselor who helps us to grow in our desire, to make it bigger and more generous. She helps us not to set a limit on our gift to the Lord. "I will follow you, Lord, but do not ask me to become this or that, to go to this country. . . ." As Saint Benedict wrote in his Rule, and Pope Benedict

XVI loved to repeat: "Put nothing before the love of Christ!" *Nihil amori Christi praeponere!*

For your prayer

Pray with Psalm 42. Ask the Lord to purify and enlarge your desire. Desire great things for yourself and for those who depend on you!

"As the deer longs for streams of water, / so my soul longs for you, O God. / My soul thirsts for God, the living God. / When can I enter and see the face of God?" (Ps 42:2–3).

Tuesday (Third Week of Lent)

GOSPEL: MT 18:21–35

Peter approached Jesus and asked him, "Lord, if my brother sins against me, how often must I forgive him? As many as seven times?" Jesus answered, "I say to you, not seven times but seventy-seven times. That is why the Kingdom of heaven may be likened to a king who decided to settle accounts with his servants. When he began the accounting, a debtor was brought before him who owed him a huge amount. Since he had no way of paying it back, his master ordered him to be sold, along with his wife, his children, and all his property, in payment of the debt. At that, the servant fell down, did him homage, and said, 'Be patient with me, and I will pay you back in full.' Moved with compassion the master of that servant let him go and forgave him the loan. When that servant had left, he found one of his fellow servants who owed him a much smaller amount. He seized him and started to choke him, demanding, 'Pay back what you owe.' Falling to his knees, his fellow servant begged him, 'Be patient with me, and I will pay you back.' But he refused. Instead, he had him put in prison until he paid back the debt. Now when his fellow servants saw what had happened, they were deeply disturbed, and went to their master and reported the whole affair. His master summoned him and said to him, 'You wicked servant! I forgave you your entire debt because you begged me to. Should you not have had pity on your fellow servant as I had pity on you?' Then in anger his master handed him over to the torturers until he should pay back the whole debt. So will my heavenly Father do to you, unless each of you forgives your brother from your heart."

(1) *Not seven times but seventy times seven*

If you like math, you will enjoy today's gospel. Peter comes with a request regarding forgiveness. Jesus has been speaking about the lost sheep and what to do when your brother sins. As an intelligent disciple, Peter has understood that the Lord comes with the good news of forgiveness.

In the times of Moses, the law of Talion was proposed in order to limit the desire of revenge. The New Moses, Jesus, brings now a new measure: "You have heard that it was said, 'An eye for an eye and a tooth for a tooth.' But I say to you, offer no resistance to one who is evil. When someone strikes you on (your) right cheek, turn the other one to him as well" (Mat 5:38–42).

Peter has heard these words of Jesus, but he needs an explanation. It is ok to forgive your brother once, twice, and even three times, but if he keeps sinning against me, am I supposed to keep offering my forgiveness? If he betrays me and says three times he doesn't know me, am I supposed to forgive me? If my friend abandons me when I am in trouble, could I forgive him?

We know the whole story and we know that Jesus will answer Peter's question with his own life, during the passion and after the resurrection, when he will encounter Peter at the lake and they will have breakfast together. But for now, the Master plays with Peter's numbers: he should not forgive seven but seventy times seven (or according to other translation, seventy seven times).

There is a great difference between the seven times of Peter and the 490 (70x7) times of Jesus. I am asked to forgive each person 490 times. In the case of my family, with six siblings and my parents, I should forgive 490 times 8, that is, 3,920 times at home. But of course, Jesus is not inviting us to count the times we forgive our brother. We are called to forgive always.

(2) *Playing with the numbers*

As a great Master, Jesus explains his answer telling us a story. Why should we forgive our brother always?

In the parable Jesus imagines for us, we find a king and two servants. The king decides to settle accounts with his people and calls one who owes him "a huge amount." The servant will be forgiven but he will be unable to forgive a friend who owes with "a much smaller amount."

In his explanation, Jesus gives some numbers: the huge amount is ten thousand talents, whereas the much smaller amount is a hundred denarii. We are not familiar with these measures. We understand better the words of Jesus if we remember that a denarius was the normal daily wage of a laborer, around four grams of silver. A hundred denarii could be like three months of work. What about the talents? A talent is a unit of coinage of high and varying value depending on its metal: gold, silver or copper. A talent would be around 21 kilograms of silver, that is around 5,250 denarii, the work of more than 14 years of work. If this is the value of one talent, just think about ten thousand talents. The debt of the servant with his king was something he could never ever pay during his whole life and in many lives. It is like an infinite debt. The numbers of Jesus speak about something really small and something huge.

Why should I forgive always my brother? Peter receives the answer in the parable. Because God has forgiven your infinite debt, you are to forgive those who offend you. The wounds we receive may be very big, but if we compare them with the forgiveness of our sins, they are like nothing. Our house can be bigger or smaller, but if you compare it with the size of the earth or of the sun, it is ridiculous.

The order of the parable is the order of our lives. We are forgiven, we experience reconciliation, and then we are able to forgive. God has the first word and establishes a dynamism of forgiveness.

(3) *Forgiveness, the repose of God*

The difference between the ten thousand talents and the hundred denarii is so huge, that we understand the indignation of the coworkers of this selfish servant. We all have a sense of injustice: *This cannot happen, this is unjust. If you are forgiven in such a way, you cannot withhold your forgiveness to this person.*

The parable finishes with a warning. The king "handed him over to the torturers until he should pay back the whole debt. So will my heavenly Father do to you, unless each of you forgives your brother from your heart."

We need to forgive because we have been forgiven. But the life of Christ reveals us that the huge love of the Father is always great than our ingratitude. Even if we don't forgive, if we ask again to the Lord, he will be patient with us and offer us a new possibility. Until we are on earth, we live in the time of God's patience. The king will forgive us again and send us home!

Why is God so persistent in his forgiveness? Saint Ambrose, who was very important in the conversion of Saint Augustine, offers an amazing explanation. Explaining God's creation, Ambrose tries to understand the meaning of his repose. God did not repose after he created the heavens or the earth, or the stars… We read that God created man and that at this point he rested. Therefore, Ambrose concludes, at that point, God rested, "having a being whose sins he could forgive" (Hexameron, IX 76).

Isn't that wonderful? God reposes and rejoices because he has someone—the human being—whose sins he can forgive. Our sin offends God, for sure. But God's mercy is so great that even our sin can be an opportunity to grow in our love. As saint Ambrose explains in other place, I can say that "my fault has become for me the price of redemption, through which Christ came to me. For me Christ tasted death. Transgression is more profitable than innocence. Innocence had made me arrogant, transgression made me humble" (*De Iacob et vita beata*, I, 21).

Finally, in a famous text we remember every year at our Easter Vigil, Ambrose thinks that "the Lord knew that Adam would fall and then be redeemed by Christ." And he exclaims joyfully and courageously: "Happy ruin, that has such a beautiful reparation!"

For your prayer

Consider the gifts of confession and plan to go to confession during this week. It would be better if you go with your family or with some friends. Afterwards, to celebrate the joy of being reconciled with God, you can have something special, ice-cream, candy...

Wednesday (Third Week of Lent)

GOSPEL: MT 5:17–19

Jesus said to his disciples: "Do not think that I have come to abolish the law or the prophets. I have come not to abolish but to fulfill. Amen, I say to you, until heaven and earth pass away, not the smallest letter or the smallest part of a letter will pass from the law, until all things have taken place. Therefore, whoever breaks one of the least of these commandments and teaches others to do so will be called least in the Kingdom of heaven. But whoever obeys and teaches these commandments will be called greatest in the Kingdom of heaven."

(1) *The gift of the Law*

Today we may be a little bit confused. During this week we are considering how Jesus encounters us at the well, the place of our desires. But in today's Gospel, he says he has not come to abolish the law but he wants us to keep even its smallest letter. Law or desire? The law seems to be what is imposed, not desired. We usually think of it as the heavy yoke of slavery.

In the Old Testament we discover a very different vision; the law is the fruit of the covenant and friendship between God and his people. On Mount Sinai, Moses hears the statutes and decrees which God teaches him. He is called to observe them in order to live and take possession of the promised land. The law is a path for Israel. Like a father guides his children, so God guides Israel through the law.

And what about the relationship between the law and our desires? We may think that without law, we are completely free, but this is completely wrong. The law is the place of freedom. Consider a musical instrument, for example, the piano. If you want to play it, you will study the "law of the music," the harmony... This law is not a reduction of my freedom to play the piano, but on the contrary, it is the necessary condition, the path to play a beautiful sonata.

This relationship happens also in the social life. If the law is not powerful there will reign the law of the most powerful. The law, in fact, protects the weak from the strong. It helps the strong to remember the value of the others and the poor to become stronger. The same happens, for example, with the "law of your love" toward your spouse and children. It is not a reduction of our freedom but a path of wisdom offered by God. Following this law our desires are called to be purified and grow.

(2) *The fulfillment of God's desire for us*

The law, given by God through Moses, is already a witness of the special love and familiarity of the Lord toward his people. God is not on his Olympus living a comfortable life, but he takes care of his people. "For what great nation is there that has gods so close to it as the LORD, our God is to us whenever we call upon him?" (Dt 4:7).

Today Jesus says he has not come to abolish but to fulfill the law. He does not bring the law written on two stones, like Moses, but written in his life and heart. He is not just a prophet of the Lord, but God himself coming to save us. What great nation is there that has a god so close to it as the Lord Jesus is to us? God is not speaking any more to us through signs, but he himself is coming. The Creator of the world and the Giver of the law is here among us. In Christ, the desire of God toward us—his desire of our happiness—is fulfilled.

(3) *The fulfillment of our desires*

What can we say then: law or desires? If Jesus has come to fulfill the law, has he come to abolish our desires? We know now that the law offers a path of growth and purification for our desires. Christ is not the enemy of our desires but its healer. He fulfills the law in order to help us to desire well. Therefore: law and desires.

The fulfillment of the law in Christ includes a greater challenge: "You have heard that it was said to your ancestors.... But I say to you" (Mt 5:21–22). Now we are called to love one another as Christ has loved us. He calls us to follow his steps: the law he has written in his life. But a greater demand requires a greater gift. To live this new way is impossible for us, unless... Christ gives us his new law, that is, the presence of his Holy Spirit in us. Now we can love as Christ has loved us, that is, with the same powerful Spirit with which he loves us.

For your prayer

Today pray the *Shema* (Hear).

Hear, O Israel! The LORD is our God, the LORD alone! Therefore you shall love the LORD, your God, with your whole heart, and with your whole being, and with your whole strength. Take to heart these words which I command you today. Keep repeating them to your children. Recite them when you are at home and when you are away, when you lie down and when you get up. Bind them on your arm as a sign and let them be as a pendant on your forehead. Write them on the doorposts of your houses and on your gates (Dt 6:4–9)

Thursday (Third Week of Lent)

GOSPEL: LK 11:14–23

[Jesus] was driving out a demon [that was] mute, and when the demon had gone out, the mute man spoke and the crowds were amazed. Some of them said, "By the power of Beelzebul, the prince of demons, he drives out demons." Others, to test him, asked him for a sign from heaven. But he knew their thoughts and said to them, "Every kingdom divided against itself will be laid waste and house will fall against house. And if Satan is divided against himself, how will his kingdom stand? For you say that it is by Beelzebul that I drive out demons. If I, then, drive out demons by Beelzebul, by whom do your own people drive them out? Therefore they will be your judges. But if it is by the finger of God that I drive out demons, then the Kingdom of God has come upon you. When a strong man fully armed guards his palace, his possessions are safe. But when one stronger than he attacks and overcomes him, he takes away the armor on which he relied and distributes the spoils. Whoever is not with me is against me, and whoever does not gather with me scatters."

(1) *Hardness of heart, smallness of desire*

At Meribah and Massah in the desert something terrible happens. In the middle of the struggles of the pilgrimage, the people of Israel prefer the onions and potatoes of Egypt rather than the presence of the Lord and his promise of a new land. With wonderful actions God had freed them from the slavery of Egypt and now they are complaining about their food.

Something similar happens to Jesus in today's Gospel. After his great miracle—driving out a demon that was mute—some among the people accuse him: "He drives out demons by the power of Beelzebul, the prince of demons."

Do not think of the logic of these reactions; there is none, but the lie enters in their hearts and they accept it. Simply, as those in Meribah and Massah, these listeners of Jesus are closed to the wonders of God. They are deaf and mute, like the man with the demon. Their hearts are hardened and they remain in the smallness of their desires. They cannot distinguish between the gift of freedom and the convenience of onions and potatoes.

(2) *The Holy Spirit, the order of my desires*

Why is Jesus able to drive out demons? Today he says he has the "finger of God," sign of the coming of the kingdom of God. Jesus expels demons because this finger of God is more powerful than all of the demons together. But what is the meaning of this "finger." Let me read the parallel text of Matthew: "But if it is by the Spirit of God that I drive out demons, then the kingdom of God has come upon you" (Mt 12:28). This "finger of God" is the Holy Spirit, present and active in the heart of Jesus.

We do not have "demons" in us like this mute man. However, our heart is full of different thoughts, desires…big and small, deep and superficial, nice and evil. This well of desire is the place where the Spirit works. We understand now the wisdom of Benedict XVI when he called us to foster a "pedagogy of desire" (7 Nov 2012).

(3) *A pedagogy of desire*

Our desires need to be guided and educated. This process implies purification and growth. In the garden of our heart we need to eradicate some weeds and help the good seeds to grow and bear fruit. As Benedict XVI put it, this purification means first of all, to discover (or perhaps rediscover) the taste of the authentic joy of life. We can learn to distinguish among the different desires according to their "after-taste." Sometimes when I follow a desire, I remain calm and more active and generous. Other times, a desire brings me to an initial delight but then to a great disappointment, bitterness, dissatisfaction, or emptiness. We need the recovery of true joy in our family, our friendships, our work...which implies self-renunciation for the sake of the other, love of knowledge, nature, and art... The pedagogy of desire begins with a declaration of war against any trivialization or superficiality of our desire. Let us help each other to discover the taste of the authentic joy of life. Heal, O Lord, and order our desires! Help us to understand which desires bring us to maturity in our marriage and family.

Together with this effort toward authentic joy, the Holy Spirit invites us to never be content with what we have achieved. The truest joy "unleashes in us the healthy restlessness that leads us to be more demanding" (Benedict XVI, 7 Nov 2012), looking for higher truth, goodness, and beauty in our relationships. Give us, Holy Spirit, a great desire for holiness. Make our hearts overflow with love.

For your prayer

Today pray to the Holy Spirit and ask his light and strength (*Veni Creator Spiritus*):

Come, Holy Spirit, Creator blest,
And in our souls take up thy rest;
Come with Thy grace and heavenly aid,
To fill the hearts which You have made.
O comforter, to You we cry,
O heavenly gift of God most high
O fount of life and fire of love,

And sweet anointing from above.
You in your sevenfold gifts are known,
You, finger of God's hand we own,
You, promise of the Father, you
Who does the tongue with power imbue.
Kindle our sense from above
And make our hearts overflow with love,
With patience firm and virtue high
The weakness of our flesh supply.
Far from us drive the foe we dread,
And grant us your peace instead.
So shall we not, with You for guide,
Turn from the path of life aside.

Friday (Third Week of Lent)

GOSPEL: MK 12:28–34

One of the scribes came to Jesus and asked him, "Which is the first of all the commandments?" Jesus replied, "The first is this: Hear, O Israel! The Lord our God is Lord alone! You shall love the Lord your God with all your heart, with all your soul, with all your mind, and with all your strength. The second is this: You shall love your neighbor as yourself. There is no other commandment greater than these." The scribe said to him, "Well said, teacher. You are right in saying, He is One and there is no other than he. And to love him with all your heart, with all your understanding, with all your strength, and to love your neighbor as yourself is worth more than all burnt offerings and sacrifices." And when Jesus saw that he answered with understanding, he said to him, "You are not far from the Kingdom of God." And no one dared to ask him any more questions.

(1) *Purifying desires: idols or the true God*

"We will never again say 'Our god,'/ to the work of our hands" (Hos 14:4). The prophet Hosea worked hard for the Lord in the pedagogy of Israel's desire. The people of God were tempted to abandon God and follow the idols and gods of the other nations. According to the law Israel could not represent God with any image, whereas the other nations had lots of idols they could see and touch. Israel was called to wait to see God's face but they were struggling to renounce the immediate possession which sight offers. They could not bear the mystery of God's hiddenness (see Pope Francis, *Lumen fidei,* 13).

As Pope Francis explains, the opposite of faith is not atheism, but idolatry. To be atheist is really difficult, almost impossible; one must deny or ignore the deepest desires and intuitions of the human heart and its restlessness. But we can follow idols. As a rabbi explained once, "idolatry is when a face addresses a face which is not a face" (Lumen fidei, 13). A human person—a real face—adores or offers his life to a piece of wood or metal, a face which is not a face, an idol. Israel had their idols and we have ours. Instead of pieces of wood who "have mouths but do not speak" (Ps 115:5), we may have an electronic device, an iPhone, iPod, iPad...which is in the center of my life.

Technology has changed our relationships. All these devices, of course, can be a wonderful way of overcoming distances and being present to my beloved (spouse, father, mother...) who is traveling or is living out of town or abroad. We all know how a conference call or just the cell-phone helps us to speak daily with our family and friends.

But we also know the devastating effect of these devices in our children and youth. The internet can become a refuge and an escape in so many cases. In order to avoid speaking with my spouse, it is easier to watch the TV during the meal which is perhaps the only time we spend together. And even if we are together as a family, our daughter can be texting her friends, absent in spirit and heart from our table. Technology has changed our relationships and has reduced dramatically our silence together. As a result, we need now new virtues that a few decades before were not so necessary. We need for example a special discipline, sacrifice, attention to what is real and solid, a strong guidance to our imagination... Otherwise these small devices will undermine our relationships.

We are what we speak. All these electronic devices tend to guide us toward individualism and selfishness. We call them I-Pad, I-Phone, I-Pod...and they isolate us in the "I," in myself. In any case, idolatry is a terrible nonsense; we worship the work of our own hands, that is, we set ourselves at the center of reality.

Idolatry fosters a comfortable and lukewarm life. An idol will not bother you nor ask you to offer your life. There is no risk of being called like Abram. But at the same time idols do not offer a path, do not give hope, do not free you from Egypt.

Hosea worked hard fostering the pedagogy of desire. Idolatry goes together with small and self-centered desires. The true God is not reduced to idols; to see him demands growth in patience and hope. Little by little the Holy Spirit enlarges our desire for God's vision.

(2) *Ask the Source, go to the essential*

The scribe wants to know. He has a great desire of understanding. He has studied the law and its more than six hundred commandments. He knows that even the law can be seen as another idol. One can just follow the law in its details, but ignore its heart and the Giver of the law. Instead of being a path for the desire, the law can serve as self-justification.

The scribe is restless. He wants to understand what is the most important thing in his life, which is the first of all the commandments. He comes to the source of living water and asks Jesus, "What is the most important thing?" Before a great exam with a lot of topics to study, the students speak about the possible questions: which topic is the most important?

The question of the scribe reveals a deep wisdom. He wants to simplify his life. Among the multiplicity of commandments and desires, he wants to grasp the essence. As the philosopher Kierkegaard wrote once, "purity of heart is to will one thing." We may remember the life of Cardinal Van Thuan, who spent thirteen years in a reeducation camp, nine in solitary confinement, under the communist government of Vietnam. When he was in prison, completely isolated, he "was reduced to the essential," that is, love: love for his friends and sheep, far away and persecuted, love for his enemies and guardians. Simplify your life. Do not complicate the things. How many things we do not need!

(3) *"You are not far from the kingdom of God"*

The question is not easy but, of course, Jesus answers it. His answer is tricky because instead of one commandment, he gives him two: Love the Lord with all your heart and love your neighbor as yourself. In his answer Jesus helps us to understand the unity of this commandment; it is only one with two faces. You cannot love the invisible God if you do not love your visible neighbors: spouse, children, siblings, parents, in-laws... But you do not really love your relatives and friends if you do not love them in the Lord. Otherwise, you will be tempted to use them, to transform them into idols.

Jesus commands us to love: "You shall love." He can command this because he has loved us in the first place and he has given us his Holy Spirit, the teacher of our heart. Our Gospel finishes with an open door, with a proposal to the scribe: "You are not far from the kingdom..." He is before you! Follow him!

For your prayer

Today we continue asking the Holy Spirit to order our heart, especially regarding our idols. Simplify my desires, my perfectionism; show me what is really essential. You can say this prayer early in the morning or at the beginning of your daily work:

Come Holy Spirit, fill the hearts of your faithful and kindle in them the fire of your love. Send forth your Spirit and they shall be created. And you shall renew the face of the earth.

Saturday (Third Week of Lent)

GOSPEL: LK 18:9–14

Jesus addressed this parable to those who were convinced of their own righteousness and despised everyone else. "Two people went up to the temple area to pray; one was a Pharisee and the other was a tax collector. The Pharisee took up his position and spoke this prayer to himself, 'O God, I thank you that I am not like the rest of humanity—greedy, dishonest, adulterous—or even like this tax collector. I fast twice a week, and I pay tithes on my whole income.' But the tax collector stood off at a distance and would not even raise his eyes to heaven but beat his breast and prayed, 'O God, be merciful to me a sinner.' I tell you, the latter went home justified, not the former; for everyone who exalts himself will be humbled, and the one who humbles himself will be exalted."

(1) *What matters first of all: God's work*

Jesus addresses his parables like the physician gives the proper medicine to the sick. This time he speaks to those who are convinced they are right and holy and are judging everyone else, that is, to us.

Today we finish the week of the Samaritan woman in which we are deepening in the hard work of the Holy Spirit in our hearts, developing his pedagogy of desire. This purification requires humility in us. Otherwise, the Spirit will be like the water trying to be mixed with oil or trying to enter into a closed bottle. He cannot work in us if we do not let him enter since he does not want slaves but friends.

Two people are praying, a Pharisee and a tax collector. Both go to encounter God and speak with him which is already something good and valuable. But only one goes home justified. We come to the adoration chapel to pray or we pray at home but this is not enough. In today's Gospel, Jesus offers another lesson in his school of prayer.

The Pharisee takes up his position. His body is already speaking before God; he is convinced of his own righteousness. Jesus offers him as a compendium of what our prayer should not be like, a prayer completely closed to God's action. The only thing we can save from this prayer are the first six words: "O God, I thank you that..." After that nice beginning, comes the disaster: "I thank you that I." Is it not good to give thanks? Should we not be grateful for our life? The problem of the Pharisee's gratitude is that it is not based on God's action ("I thank you that You") but on his own works. Even worse, his prayer begins with his distance from the others: "Thank you because I am not like the others." In this way, the best of the prayer—gratitude—is transformed into the worst action of pride and hidden complaint. The corruption of the best things is the worst of the corruptions. Corruptio optimi, pessima.

Jesus wants us to believe that the Pharisee is not lying. He really is fasting twice a week, paying tithes, and many other good works. All these, of course, are great things. But like the worm in the apple, pride and judgment are destroying his works. Without humility he is unable to participate in the compassionate gaze of Christ; he cannot be perfect, that is merciful. Whatever he does or endures will have no reward since he has already been rewarded. He does not live under the eyes of the Father!

What about the tax collector? "O God, be merciful to me a sinner." The beginning is similar: "O God!" But the length and style of his prayer and the message of his body (not raising his eyes but beating his breast) is quite different. Learn a first lesson for your prayer: Be brief. You do not have to speak a lot, but rather to hear a lot. Be brief in your prayer, repeat it, and stay in silence. The main word will be God's.

The second lesson of this prayer marks the decisive difference with the Pharisee's prayer: Pay attention to the action of God and only then, after this, to your action. "O God, (you) be merciful." In my prayer what is most important is not what I will do but what the Lord will do in me. Of course, my action is decisive, but only after considering God's work. And what is my action? "Be merciful to me, a sinner."

(2) *Self-knowledge, fruit of God's knowledge*

In his short lesson in the school of prayer, Jesus shows some of the fruits of prayer. When I acknowledge and proclaim God's work in me, I deepen in the mystery of God and thus in self-knowledge. The more we know God and his mercy, the more we can understand ourselves and our desires.

Who is God? We find the answer in the prayer of the tax collector; God is merciful and forgiving. This sinner does not raise his eyes since he knows the compassionate eyes of the Father are looking at him. He remains in the last place because he remembers Jesus has chosen the lowest place and has given his blood for him. He beats his breast which has been closed to the diligent work of the Holy Spirit.

And who am I? I am the apple of the eyes of the Father. My price is the body and blood of Jesus Christ, the Son of God. My future is to reflect the glory of Christ through the action of the Holy Spirit.

In our prayer, God reveals himself and thus he reveals man to himself. We understand who is God and who am I.

(3) *O God, I thank you*

Today you can develop your gratitude, the virtue of sonship. The Pharisee has taught us that even the best prayer, gratitude, can be useless if it lacks humility. "I give you thanks because I am not like the others." This sick "gratitude" is transformed into a subtle complaint against the others (tax collectors and "the rest of humanity, greedy, dishonest, and adulterous") and finally against God, who has created them. In his gratitude he pretends to be even better and higher than God and he judges him. The Pharisee adores himself and prays to himself.

"One went justified." The tax collector does not want to justify himself through his pride. He wants to stop sinning and he knows that "everyone who exalts himself, will be humbled, and the one who humbles himself will be exalted." For that reason, in his petition we discover trust in the Lord and gratitude. "O God thank you for being merciful to me a sinner." Together with him we can give thanks with our own words: "O God, I give you thanks for the others, for they are not like me. Thank you for my wife, my children, my parents… Bless them!"

For your prayer

Do you want to grow in this understanding? Today you can pray again the Litany of Humility, as we did last week (see Tuesday, Second Week of Lent). You can also repeat during the day the so-called Prayer of Jesus: "Jesus, Son of God, have mercy on me, the sinner."

THE BLIND: OUR BOLDNESS

(FOURTH WEEK OF LENT)

Fourth Sunday of Lent (A)

GOSPEL: JN 9:1–41

As Jesus passed by he saw a man blind from birth. His disciples asked him, "Rabbi, who sinned, this man or his parents, that he was born blind?" Jesus answered, "Neither he nor his parents sinned; it is so that the works of God might be made visible through him. We have to do the works of the one who sent me while it is day. Night is coming when no one can work. While I am in the world, I am the light of the world." When he had said this, he spat on the ground and made clay with the saliva, and smeared the clay on his eyes, and said to him, "Go wash in the Pool of Siloam" —which means Sent—. So he went and washed, and came back able to see.

His neighbors and those who had seen him earlier as a beggar said, "Isn't this the one who used to sit and beg?" Some said, "It is," but others said, "No, he just looks like him." He said, "I am." So they said to him, "So how were your eyes opened?" He replied, "The man called Jesus made clay and anointed my eyes and told me, 'Go to Siloam and wash.' So I went there and washed and was able to see." And they said to him, "Where is he?" He said, "I don't know."

They brought the one who was once blind to the Pharisees. Now Jesus had made clay and opened his eyes on a sabbath. So then the Pharisees also asked him how he was able to see. He said to them, "He put clay on my eyes, and I washed, and now I can see." So some of the Pharisees said, "This man is not from God, because he does not keep the sabbath." But others said, "How can a sinful man do such signs?" And there was a division among them. So they said to the blind man again, "What do you have to say about him, since he opened your eyes?" He said, "He is a prophet."

Now the Jews did not believe that he had been blind and gained his sight until they summoned the parents of the one who had gained his sight. They asked them, "Is this your son, who you say was born blind? How does he now see?" His parents answered and said, "We know that this is our son and that he was born blind. We do not know how he sees now, nor do we know who opened his eyes. Ask him, he is of age; he can speak for himself." His parents said this because they were afraid of the Jews, for the Jews had already agreed that if anyone acknowledged him as the Messiah, he would be expelled from the synagogue. For this reason his parents said, "He is of age; question him."

So a second time they called the man who had been blind and said to him, "Give God the praise! We know that this man is a sinner." He replied, "If he is a sinner, I do not know. One thing I do know is that I was blind and now I see." So they said to him, "What did he do to you? How did he open your eyes?" He answered them, "I told you already and you did not listen. Why do you want to hear it again? Do you want to become his disciples, too?" They ridiculed him and said, "You are that man's disciple; we are disciples of Moses! We know that God spoke to Moses, but we do not know where this one is from." The man answered and said to them, "This is what is so amazing, that you do not know where he is from, yet he opened my eyes. We know that God does not listen to sinners, but if one is devout and does his will, he listens to him. It is unheard of that anyone ever opened the eyes of a person born blind. If this man were not from God, he would not be able to do anything." They answered and said to him, "You were born totally in sin, and are you trying to teach us?" Then they threw him out.

When Jesus heard that they had thrown him out, he found him and said, "Do you believe in the Son of Man?" He answered and said,

"Who is he, sir, that I may believe in him?" Jesus said to him, "You have seen him, the one speaking with you is he." He said, "I do believe, Lord," and he worshiped him. Then Jesus said, "I came into this world for judgment, so that those who do not see might see, and those who do see might become blind."

Some of the Pharisees who were with him heard this and said to him, "Surely we are not also blind, are we?" Jesus said to them, "If you were blind, you would have no sin; but now you are saying, 'We see,' so your sin remains.

Rejoice! Today we celebrate a special Sunday of Lent. In the middle of our path toward Easter we are invited to remember the action of God and rejoice: "Laetare!" Be glad because your ash is being transformed by the Holy Spirit.

Rejoice! This is the first word of the Gospel, pronounced by Gabriel to Mary. To be Christian, a disciple of Jesus, is to be filled with this joy: God with us, God saves. This joy was the conversion of the thirsty Samaritan woman and today this joy will be the gift of the man blind from birth.

(1) *Rejoice: Christ is light of the world*

Who sinned? Who is guilty? Seeing a man blind from birth, the disciples are scandalized. Without light this poor life has no colors, no order, no safety nor cleanliness but only night, fear, and confusion. Trying to understand this evil they look for the guilty one; perhaps he or his parents sinned.

Who sinned? Why is this human person without knowledge and living such a pitiful life? These were the thoughts of a young disciple—a novice—while he was taking care and feeding a poor handicapped man in the "House of the Divine Providence." Why, O Lord? He was even unable to open his mouth and receive the soup. His eyes were completely lost. An old sister happened to cross the hallway and looked at the disciple. "Wait a minute. Do you know why this man is here? Do you know why? He is here 'so that the works of God might be made visible through him.' What are the works and glory of God? Love, charity, patience. This man is here and whoever gets close to him grows in love and mercy. He is a generator of mercy in the world!"

Who sinned? That's not the question. Jesus answers the disciples explaining to them the sense of this suffering. "It is so that the works of God might be made visible through him." Instead of looking immediately for the guilty cause of your suffering, try to understand its meaning, the opportunity opened to you through it. Sometimes, of course, you will have to deal with the guilty one but do not let resentment stay in your heart.

Jesus does not speak any more but he acts. He makes clay with the saliva and smears the clay on the useless eyes of the blind man. For some Fathers of the Church this mysterious sign of Jesus is connected with Creation (Gn 2). In the beginning, God created man, modeling clay with his hands and giving him the spirit of life. After sin, this clay was deformed with death and illnesses, among which is blindness. Today, Jesus models again this clay, recreating it. Creation was awaiting the hands of Jesus. With him there is a new beginning, a new creation. These eyes, blind during so many years, were created to see the beauty of the world. My family life, my work, my study. . . blind or deaf for years, is called to this fulfillment!

We can understand very well that the news spread over the city very quickly, even if it was sabbath that day. His neighbors and the people of the city had seen him blind for so many years. But the news of the miracle also spread due to the joy of the blind man. Can you imagine his joy? Until he encountered Jesus, he had been living in a complete darkness. Without light we experience fear, cold, and sadness. Light helps us to order our room or our office, to discover the beauty of the world, to avoid any fear, to see the shapes and colors of the things, to contemplate the face of the person. . . The ex-blind man can not remain silent: "Look at me! I was blind, but now I see!" And his first steps will be wonder after wonder, surprise after surprise. I guess he went quickly to see the face of his parents since until then he had only touched it with his hands. Imagine the joy of this moment. Do you think that the blind man slept a minute that night? He wanted to go to all his friends and tell them: "I see!" He wanted to spend hours with his beloved, with his family, contemplating them, trying to recover the time he had lost and preparing his heart for the awe of his first sunrise.

(2) *He is of age: question him*

Soon the huge joy of the blind man is tested. The Pharisees do not share the wonder of the people. They do not want to see and believe so they try to find out what has happened. In this case there is only one solution: this man was not blind. He is another person, similar perhaps, but he is not—he cannot be—the man blind from birth, since it is unheard that anyone ever opened the eyes of a person born blind. This miracle simply cannot happen. They have to explain it in another way.

They do not want to believe. "Night is coming." Like the rich man before Lazarus, even if a dead man is risen, the rich man will not change. And even if a man blind from birth sees, they will not believe. "The light came into the world, but people preferred darkness to light" (John 3:19).

The judgment continues. They ask the parents and they testify he is their son and he was blind. But they are afraid and they do not risk their lives: "He is of age: question him." They say something really true: "Our son is prepared for the test of faith; go and ask him."

The Pharisees go and question him again. You can meditate on this beautiful dialogue between light and darkness, between the ex-blind man transformed by Jesus and the Pharisees closed to him. Finally they throw him out. Then Jesus questions him.

Jesus wants to give the blind man thanks for risking his life for him before the Pharisees and wants to confront him with the great question: "Do you believe in the Son of Man?" (Jn 9:35). This moment is the second encounter with Jesus and the first time the blind man sees his face. The blind man recognizes the voice who gave him light and now also sees his face and his hands, no longer dirty with the clay. Imagine the beauty of this encounter. The man born blind exclaims joyfully: "Lord, I believe!" (see Jn 9:38), giving voice to all believers.

We are of age. And we are questioned by the Lord: Do you believe in me? No matter if you are a high schooler, a student at college, single, dating, just married, already a grandparent. Prepare yourself to answer the question: Who has healed you? Who has given you this new joy and light? Prepare yourself to risk your prestige and your life for Christ. Become children of the light!

(3) *You now see: follow me!*

The light expels any fear and makes us bold and courageous. When we encounter Jesus we want to follow him and share with others the joy of his friendship. The Samaritan woman was successful in her apostolate in the town. The blind man was insulted and thrown out because he was courageous.

Looking at him we are called to great gifts and to risk our life for Christ. It can be helpful to remember the resolution of Maria Teresa Gonzalez-Quevedo when she was in high school: "I have decided to become a saint." "Teresita," now servant of God, wanted to offer the best years of her life: "Do not give the world the best of your life. Jesus wants the gift of youth, with all its joys and dreams."

Then, following an inner desire, Teresita asked Mary: "O My Mother, grant me the grace of a religious vocation!" She wanted to follow Jesus closely in poverty, obedience, and chastity. "While I was coming out—she said to one of her friends later on—I was terribly scared thinking: And what if Our Lady really grants me this grace?"

For your prayer

Offer your life together with the man born blind and now healed by Jesus.

Take, Lord, and receive all my liberty, my memory, my understanding and my entire will: all that I have and possess. You have given all to me. To you, O Lord, I return it. All is yours. Dispose of it wholly according to your will. Give me your love and your grace, for this is sufficient for me.

NICODEMUS: OUR BOLDNESS

(FOURTH WEEK OF LENT)

Fourth Sunday of Lent (B)

GOSPEL: JN 3:14–21

Jesus said to Nicodemus: "Just as Moses lifted up the serpent in the desert, so must the Son of Man be lifted up, so that everyone who believes in him may have eternal life."

For God so loved the world that he gave his only Son, so that everyone who believes in him might not perish but might have eternal life. For God did not send his Son into the world to condemn the world, but that the world might be saved through him. Whoever believes in him will not be condemned, but whoever does not believe has already been condemned, because he has not believed in the name of the only Son of God. And this is the verdict, that the light came into the world, but people preferred darkness to light, because their works were evil. For everyone who does wicked things hates the light and does not come toward the light, so that his works might not be exposed. But whoever lives the truth comes to the light, so that his works may be clearly seen as done in God.

Laetare! Rejoice! This is the exclamation that permeates today's liturgy and the whole week. In the middle of our Lenten path, as a midterm exam, the Lord invites us to rejoice. In our transformation from ash to water, we rejoice because the Holy Spirit is at work, recreating us.

(1) *A night conversation with Jesus*

In the midway of our Lent, we contemplate a dialogue between Jesus and one of his disciples, Nicodemus, a Pharisee and member of the Sanhedrin, who comes in the darkness. The night is the time of intimacy, the time to be with the beloved.

Nicodemus comes during the night, probably because he is not sure about Jesus and he is afraid to be accused by other Pharisees. It seems he hesitates to proclaim his faith in Jesus because he is fearful of others. Jesus is very patient with his friends. The day will come in which Nicodemus will risk his life with Jesus, but in the meanwhile, the Master is patient and welcome him during the night.

Nicodemus has studied a lot. He is a wise man looking for the truth. Having heard about Jesus of Nazareth, he wants to know if he is the One, the Messiah. Why did Nicodemus acknowledge the Christ and other pharisees rejected him? All his studies and research would be sterile if he does not recognize Jesus. Now, before him, we see that all his efforts were not emptiness. Unlike other Pharisees, he is able to discover Jesus as the Messiah because he was searching for the truth with a pure heart. As saint Bonaventure recommends in a famous prayer, Nicodemus has developed reading with repentance, research with the impulse of wonder, prudence with the ability to surrender to joy, action united to religion, learning with love, intelligence with humility, study sustained by divine grace, and thought with the wisdom inspired by God (cf. Saint Bonaventure, *Itinerarium Mentis in Deum*).

Today we are invited to rejoice with Nicodemus. Jesus welcomes us whenever we visit him. In our adoration chapel he is waiting for us 24/ 7, at 2am or at noon; but also at home, at work, in the hospital or at the school, resting or practicing sport, he is always at hand.

(2) *God so loved the world*

As a fruit of his personal path, Nicodemus will recognize Jesus as the Messiah, the one whom the prophets and the whole Scripture announced. He will discover in him the fulfilment of the word of God.

Jesus helps Nicodemus explaining him the meaning of a very important miracle of Moses in the desert. When the people of Israel complained against Moses, God sent them snakes that bit them so that many died (Numbers 21:4–9). Then, after Moses' prayer, the Lord asked him to make a bronze serpent and mount it on a pole. Everyone who had been bitten looked at it and recovered.

What happened in the desert was a sign of what will happen when the Son of Man will be lifted up. Jesus is preparing Nicodemus to the time of the Cross. When Nicodemus will witness the passion and death of Christ, he will remember this dialogue during the night.

Rejoice, Nicodemus! Rejoice because Moses made a serpent of bronze in the desert and now God has sent his Son as a New Moses. He will hang on the Cross and those who look at him with faith will be healed.

Today we are invited to rejoice as we consider the wonders of the Lord. Jesus helped Nicodemus remember the works of Moses in the desert and its fulfilment in him. Today's readings invite us to remember the works of Moses and Jesus and its fulfilment in our family life. God so love the world that he gave his only Son! Whenever we remember these words we are invited to rejoice.

To think of God gives joy. Sometimes we think of God and we have no joy because we don't think well of God but we follow our idols, our own opinions. To think of God gives joy to our heart because God so love the world... This is the principal proclamation of the Church, which remains unchanged down the ages. When we encounter Jesus Christ, we understand our life is marked by love, by the infinite love of God.

(3) *God of courage and strength*

To think of God gives joy and also courage. During his first encounters with Jesus, Nicodemus was a secret friend. Saint John mentions him three times in his gospel. The first is today's gospel (Jn 3). The second time we know about Nicodemus, we see him defending Jesus before the Sanhedrin (Jn 7:45–52). Thirdly, after the death of Jesus, he will come with Joseph of Arimathea to bury his body (Jn 19:38–42).

To think of God gives courage. Nicodemus started his friendship with Jesus in the darkness of the night and he will finish proclaiming by day his love and faith in Jesus. Finally he will be able to risk his life for Jesus. If Judah the Iscariot walks from light into darkness, Nicodemus will come from darkness to light and he will become a beacon of hope.

As a matter of fact, we celebrate Nicodemus' holiness on August 31, along with Saint Joseph of Arimathea. The feast day used to be celebrated on August 3, which, according to a tradition, was the anniversary of the finding of his relics, along with those of Stephen the protomartyr and other two saints.

Nicodemus walked from fear to courage. The Pharisee invites us to risk our life for Jesus. How many fears prevent us from proclaiming the Gospel of life! Come, Holy Spirit, give us strength to share our faith and to overcome any shame of Christ. We know that in our struggle against sin we have not yet "resisted to the point of shedding blood" (Hebrews 12:4). Saint Nicodemus, help us to be proud of our faith!

For your prayer

Ask the Holy Spirit the gift of fortitude with the words of Saint Alphonsus Liguori:

Grant me, Lord, the gift of fortitude, so that I may overcome courageously all the assaults of the devil, and all the dangers of this world which threaten the salvation of my soul.

THE MERCIFUL FATHER: OUR BOLDNESS

(FOURTH WEEK OF LENT)

Fourth Sunday of Lent (*C*)

GOSPEL: LK 15:1–3, 11–32

Tax collectors and sinners were all drawing near to listen to Jesus, but the Pharisees and scribes began to complain, saying, "This man welcomes sinners and eats with them." So to them Jesus addressed this parable. "A man had two sons, and the younger son said to his father, 'Father, give me the share of your estate that should come to me.' So the father divided the property between them. After a few days, the younger son collected all his belongings and set off to a distant country where he squandered his inheritance on a life of dissipation. When he had freely spent everything, a severe famine struck that country, and he found himself in dire need. So he hired himself out to one of the local citizens who sent him to his farm to tend the swine. And he longed to eat his fill of the pods on which the swine fed, but nobody gave him any. Coming to his senses he thought, 'How many of my father's hired workers have more than enough food to eat, but here am I, dying from hunger. I shall get up and go to my father and I shall say to him, "Father, I have sinned against heaven and against you. I no longer deserve to be called your son; treat me as you would treat one of your hired workers."' So he got up and went back to his father. While he was still a long way off, his father caught sight of him, and was filled with compassion. He ran to his son, embraced him and kissed him. His son said to him, 'Father, I have sinned against heaven and against you; I no longer deserve to be called your son.' But his father ordered his servants, 'Quickly, bring the finest robe and put it on him; put a ring on his finger and sandals on his feet. Take the fattened calf and slaughter it. Then let us celebrate with a feast, because this son of mine was dead, and has come to life again; he was lost, and has been found.' Then the celebration began.

Now the older son had been out in the field and, on his way back, as he neared the house, he heard the sound of music and dancing. He called one of the servants and asked what this might mean. The servant said to him, 'Your brother has returned and your father has slaughtered the fattened calf because he has him back safe and sound.' He became angry, and when he refused to enter the house, his father came out and pleaded with him. He said to his father in reply, 'Look, all these years I served you and not once did I disobey your orders; yet you never gave me even a young goat to feast on with my friends. But when your son returns who swallowed up your property with prostitutes, for him you slaughter the fattened calf.' He said to him,

'My son, you are here with me always; everything I have is yours. But now we must celebrate and rejoice, because your brother was dead and has come to life again; he was lost and has been found.'"

(1) *A parable that changed the cosmos*

Today's gospel marks a milestone in the history of humanity. As Benedict XVI put it a few years ago, "after Jesus has told us of the merciful Father, things are no longer as they were before" (14 March 2010). The world cannot be the same!

The Fourth Sunday of Lent is always an invitation to rejoice. *Laetare*! In this year, the reasons for joy are evident: we hear the parable of the "prodigal father" and we rejoice because Jesus reveals the face and heart of God. Our Creator is our Father, one who suffers when we get lost and rejoices when we return, one who suffers also when we remain sadly in his house.

After Jesus has given us this parable, the world is not the same. When we hear today's gospel of mercy, our life, our family relationships, our work...need to change.

We need to be grateful to the Pharisees and scribes because their complaints moved Jesus to imagine this parable. Tax collectors and sinners were drawing near to listen to Jesus. He was not rejecting them but he was welcoming and was eating and drinking with them.

The complaints of the Jews could be reasonable. What are you doing, Jesus? Are you telling us that these sinners are in a good place? Are you trying to justify them? But Jesus never tells the sinners: "It is good what you are doing. I love you. Continue as before." Jesus welcomes the sinners, eats with them and calls them to conversion, to a new way of life: "Go and sin no more. Come back to the Father. Rejoice and receive his embrace! Rejoice and change!"

(2) *Amazing grace*

Today Jesus speaks about a father with two sons. One abandons him, rejects his identity and goes far to squander his inheritance living in dissipation. The other lives with him and works hard, but his heart is far from his father. He works like an obedient slave, not as a son.

Both, the younger and the older sons, are called to be embraced by the father. Both have an immature relationship with their father: one through rebellion, the other through childish obedience. Both need to experience forgiveness and mercy. They need to recognize the unconditional love of the Father, which is greater than our wretchedness (the younger) but also than our own merit (the older).

These two brothers are called to reconciliation in a different way. They need to throw themselves into the arms of the Father and be regenerated by his merciful love.

Rembrandt has given us a wonderful image of the return of the younger son. We see the child kneeling before his elderly father. He comes back dirty, with torn and worn out clothes. His inside is destroyed, hopeless, empty... Is there any hope for someone like him? The father embraces him and gives him a new beginning.

What about the older son? Rembrandt has also painted him, with rich garments, looking at his brother with anger. His inside is full of pride, envy and confusion. Is there any hope for someone like him? The father will call him to rejoice with him and welcome his brother.

The experience of these two brothers is the encounter with an amazing grace. We can recognize here the beautiful words of John Newton: "Amazing grace! How sweet the sound that saved a wretch like me. I once was lost, but now am found, was blind but now I see." The amazing grace of the Father gives light to the two brothers: from rebellion and from childish obedience, they are called to rejoice as sons, beloved unconditionally.

(3) *The "duty" of joy*

Jesus finishes his parable speaking about the older son. After a long day working in the field, he nears the house and hears music. When he finds out the news, he becomes angry and doesn't want to enter the house. He is confused and envious because he doesn't understand his father. "Why are you so strange, father? You reward your disobedient son and you forget me!"

The answer of the father is a commandment: "Now we must celebrate and rejoice." Joy is our duty. We *must* celebrate and share God's joy. Saint Paul will insist in this duty in many occasions: "Rejoice in the Lord always. I shall say it again: rejoice! Your kindness should be known to all. The Lord is near" (Philippians 4:4–5).

"Now we must rejoice." Maybe this is one of the toughest commandments of Jesus. We have many reasons to complain and be sad. Why should I rejoice?

Many times, like the older brother we struggle in our joy. We complain, we become envious and angry when we see that someone close to us prosper or get closer to the Lord.

Why should we rejoice when our brother is blessed, when he comes to life again? Our envy and complains can only be overcome when we receive the embrace of the Father. Our anger against our brother is a symptom which reveals a problem in our relationship with the Father. If we experience frequently his mercy, then we will rejoice when our brother comes back. We will rejoice when new people come to Sunday Mass and when we see someone in "our" pew.

For your prayer

Spend one or two minutes giving to the Lord your reasons to rejoice.

Think about your experiences as younger and older brother, about your rebellions and your obedience as "slave."

Make a commitment to be more welcoming and smiling at Sunday

Mass.

Monday (Fourth Week of Lent)

GOSPEL: JN 4:43–54

At that time Jesus left [Samaria] for Galilee. For Jesus himself testified that a prophet has no honor in his native place. When he came into Galilee, the Galileans welcomed him, since they had seen all he had done in Jerusalem at the feast; for they themselves had gone to the feast. Then he returned to Cana in Galilee, where he had made the water wine. Now there was a royal official whose son was ill in Capernaum. When he heard that Jesus had arrived in Galilee from Judea, he went to him and asked him to come down and heal his son, who was near death. Jesus said to him, "Unless you people see signs and wonders, you will not believe." The royal official said to him, "Sir, come down before my child dies." Jesus said to him, "You may go; your son will live." The man believed what Jesus said to him and left. While the man was on his way back, his slaves met him and told him that his boy would live. He asked them when he began to recover. They told him, "The fever left him yesterday, about one in the afternoon." The father realized that just at that time Jesus had said to him, "Your son will live," and he and his whole household came to believe. Now this was the second sign Jesus did when he came to Galilee from Judea.

During this week we will be reading the Gospel of Saint John, full of deep insights, and we will deal with the mystery of Jesus, Light of the World.

(1) *The light of the pilgrim: walk and you will see*

The two first miracles—signs—of Jesus found in the Gospel of Saint John happened in Cana of Galilee. Both give life to a family. The first time through the intercession of Mary, Jesus made the water wine. Today through the intercession of the father of the family, he heals a child who is about to die. Jesus has come to heal our family, to give new hope to our relationships. With his light he wants to reorder and illuminate the way we build our relationships.

Do you ride your bicycle during the night? It can be dangerous if there is traffic. You may ride early in the morning or late in the afternoon and need a light on your bicycle. There are, of course, the lamps with their own batteries. But you can also find the lamps which depend on a dynamo system, that is, that require no batteries but depend on your own energy and movement. In this case the lamp will begin to light when you begin to pedal. Stopped there will be no light. But when you begin to move forward, the light will show the path.

Jesus asks something similar to this when the royal official comes and intercedes for his child. "You may go. Your son will live." Do not wait here. Just begin to walk toward your home and you will see. Jesus finds obedience and faith in this man. "The man believed what Jesus said to him and left. While the man was on his way back, his slaves met him and told him that his boy would live." Do not remain alone and stuck, waiting for nothing. Jesus will give no light for the lazy and slothful. Do you need light from the Lord? Begin to walk! The light of Jesus is light for the pilgrim (see Saint Augustine, Homilies).

(2) *"And his whole household began to believe"*

The light of Jesus is light for the pilgrim family. The royal officer is asking for his whole family. If he does not ask, the child would not have lived. The miracle of Jesus transforms all his relationships: not only with his son, but also with his wife—the mother of his son—and with the other children, the siblings of his son.

The light I receive is not only for myself. It is not mine but ours.

The Gospel adds that the royal officer "and his whole household came to believe." This leadership is the mission of the father in the family. In a special way, he is called to be the light that prevents his children from remaining in darkness, sleeping, hiding from the day and from the challenge of risking their lives.

(3) *A new light, a new creation*

We can finish considering the first reading in which the prophet Isaiah proclaims the creation of new heavens and a new earth:

> The former things shall not be remembered / nor come to mind. / Instead, shout for joy and be glad forever / in what I am creating. / Indeed, I am creating Jerusalem to be a joy / and its people to be a delight; / I will rejoice in Jerusalem / and exult in my people. (Is 65:17–19)

The light of Christ brought by the father to his family implies a new way of living together. This new life is Jesus' promise. When the whole household comes to believe, they begin to look at each other in a different way: spouse to spouse, father to son, son to father... Their relationships are no longer based on pleasure, utility, or resentment but on the gift of themselves. This way of relating is the light of Christ. And of course, we receive this light slowly, step by step. Little by little our eyes are transformed and we can look at our family with the great hope of God.

For your prayer

The light of the pilgrim is not given in a moment but step by step. We cannot receive and understand the whole light of the itinerary in our life. We cannot carry all the bread and water we will need for the two week pilgrimage. It is too much. Today we can pray: "Give us this day our daily bread." Read the Daily Decalogue of Pope John XXIII,

"Only for Today."

(1) *Only for Today, I will seek to live the livelong day positively without wishing to solve the problems of my life all at once.*

(2) *Only for Today, I will take the greatest care of my appearance: I will dress modestly; I will not raise my voice; I will be courteous in my behavior; I will not criticize anyone; I will not claim to improve or to discipline anyone except myself.*

(3) *Only for Today, I will be happy in the certainty that I was created to be happy, not only in the other world but also in this one.*

(4) *Only for Today, I will adapt to circumstances, without requiring all circumstances to be adapted to my own wishes.*

(5) *Only for Today, I will devote ten minutes of my time to good reading, remembering that just as food is necessary to the life of the body, so good reading is necessary to the life of the soul.*

(6) *Only for Today, I will do one good deed and not tell anyone about it.*

(7) *Only for Today, I will do at least one thing I do not like doing; and if my feelings are hurt, I will make sure that no one notices.*

(8) *Only for Today, I will make a plan for myself: I may not follow it to the letter, but I will make it. And I will be on guard against two evils: hastiness and indecision.*

(9) *Only for Today, I will firmly believe, despite appearances, that the good providence of God cares for me as no one else who exists in this world.*

(10) *Only for Today, I will have no fears. In particular, I will not be afraid to enjoy what is beautiful and to believe in goodness. Indeed, for twelve hours I can certainly do what might cause me consternation were I to believe I had to do it all my life.*

To conclude: here is an all-embracing resolution: "I want to be kind, today and always, to everyone."

In this way, we can put Pope John's hope for every Christian into practice. We are called to be a spark of light, a core of love, life-giving leaven in the mass. The more we are so, the more we will live, in our innermost depths, in communion with God. (Cardinal Tarcisio Bertone, October 11, 2006, Memorial Mass of Blessed John XXIII)

Tuesday (Fourth Week of Lent)

GOSPEL: JN 5:1–16

There was a feast of the Jews, and Jesus went up to Jerusalem. Now there is in Jerusalem at the Sheep Gate a pool called in Hebrew Bethesda, with five porticoes. In these lay a large number of ill, blind, lame, and crippled. One man was there who had been ill for thirty-eight years. When Jesus saw him lying there and knew that he had been ill for a long time, he said to him, "Do you want to be well?" The sick man answered him, "Sir, I have no one to put me into the pool when the water is stirred up; while I am on my way, someone else gets down there before me." Jesus said to him, "Rise, take up your mat, and walk." Immediately the man became well, took up his mat, and walked.

Now that day was a sabbath. So the Jews said to the man who was cured, "It is the sabbath, and it is not lawful for you to carry your mat." He answered them, "The man who made me well told me, 'Take up your mat and walk.'" They asked him, "Who is the man who told you, 'Take it up and walk'?" The man who was healed did not know who it was, for Jesus had slipped away, since there was a crowd there. After this Jesus found him in the temple area and said to him, "Look, you are well; do not sin any more, so that nothing worse may happen to you." The man went and told the Jews that Jesus was the one who had made him well. Therefore, the Jews began to persecute Jesus because he did this on a sabbath.

(1) *A new measure of light*

FROM ASH TO WATER

How much love, how much light have we received? We know we receive the light of the pilgrim, that is, a light that does not blind us but helps us to see better. But what is the measure of this light?

In Jerusalem, in the pool of the five porticoes called Bethesda, the water was healing only once in a while. This sick man has been ill for thirty-eight years, more than Jesus' life, and nobody has helped him. Jesus looks at him with pity. Thirty eight years! He has already lost any hope. He is too slow and the others are always before him in the pool.

"Do you want to be well?" Perhaps, like this sick man, you have also lost any hope of being healed. How many years struggling with your marriage? How much time trying to overcome this vice? How many months asking the Lord for an answer regarding your vocation?

After so many years and after coming to the "pool" and begging, praying to God to heal this marriage or this sin, or this uncertainty, why does Jesus not arrive now? Is there something else needed? Is the hope false? How can we know or believe or hope that Jesus is coming now to heal and to save?

Today! Today Jesus wants to begin this path of healing. The Book of Revelation reminds us of the great desire of Jesus' heart: "Behold, I stand at the door and knock. If anyone hears my voice and opens the door, [then] I will enter his house and dine with him, and he with me" (Rev 3:20). Today Jesus is knocking at your door! If only you hear him and open the door of your heart!

Today, after so many years waiting, Jesus arrives and asks this sick man: "Do you want to be well?" The question may surprise us. Of course, he wants! Otherwise, what is he doing here? But Jesus wants him to pronounce his petition.

This man has been his whole life waiting but the water of the pool of Bethesda is not generous. Only once in a while there is a movement. Now Christ has arrived. He is the source of the living water, the light of the world (see Jn 4:7). He brings a new measure of water and light: a generous and abundant measure.

In today's first reading, Ezekiel prophesies a future abundance of grace. From the side of the temple flows a great river of grace. "I saw water flowing out from under the threshold of the temple toward the east" (Ez 47:1). This water flows and empties into the sea, the salt waters, making it fresh. Wherever the river flows there is abundant fish. Along both banks of the river fruit trees of every kind grow. Now Christ has arrived. He is the new temple, the new presence of God with his people. He brings with him a river of grace, the gift of the Spirit.

For that reason, when Jesus dies on the cross, one soldier thrusts his lance into his side and blood and water flow out (see Jn 19:32–37). When Saint John sees this, he is amazed: "An eyewitness has testified, and his testimony is true; he knows that he is speaking the truth, so that you also may [come to] believe" (Jn 19:35). The great river described by Ezekiel flows from the temple, that is, from the heart of Christ.

(2) *Loyalty to the one who saved you*

It is the sabbath when Jesus asks the sick man to rise, take up his mat, and walk (see Jn 5). And this fact is a test for this man. Should he obey Jesus and walk or remain quiet according to the law? To break the law of the sabbath was dangerous and was only reasonable if Jesus was really the Messiah, the One we were waiting for. The beginning is good: he takes up his mat and begins to walk. But then the Jews remind him he is not allowed to do that on the sabbath. And finally the new walking man tries to justify himself and to appear just before them. "It is not my fault, but of the one who healed me." Out of fear, from his initial obedience to Jesus, he finishes in betrayal. He goes to the Jews and tells them "that Jesus was the one who had made him well."

Be loyal to Christ. This poor man is afraid and finally he rejects

Jesus, his Savior. He prefers to avoid persecution, rather than follow Christ. He is not like the blind man who courageously defends Jesus. But, dear friend, the one who has cured you and has made you able to walk, will he not be powerful enough to save you from these men and give you life again?

(3) *Never enough, never too late*

How much love, how much light have we received? There is a river of grace coming from the heart of Christ. His measure is a good measure, packed together, shaken down, and overflowing. Do not be satisfied with less. What will be our adequate answer? Remember that "when love says It is enough, it dies." The great love of Jesus waits for a generous answer. Do not say: "Enough" in your love to your spouse and to your kids. Do not be satisfied just with a comfortable life. Have great desires of holiness in your vocation! Ask Jesus to teach you gratitude and generosity.

Never is it enough and never is it "too late." "Look you are well; do not sin any more, so that nothing worse may happen to you." Jesus is always offering a path of conversion. Perhaps you think it is too late for you or for your wife or children. Never is it too late. Jesus is always calling: "Dear sick man. After thirty-eight years you received the great gift of encountering me and you were able to walk. But right after your healing, your new life was broken by fear; you rejected me. Do not be afraid. Be humble. Come to me and I will give you rest."

For your prayer

Do not say "Enough!" Do not reserve yourself. Pray with Saint Ignatius of Loyola:

Lord Jesus, teach me to be generous, teach me to serve you as I should, to give and not to count the cost, to fight and not to heed the wounds, to toil and not to seek for rest, to labour and ask not for reward, save that of knowing that I do your most holy will (St. Ignatius of Loyola).

Wednesday (Fourth Week of Lent)

GOSPEL: JN 5:17–30

Jesus answered the Jews: "My Father is at work until now, so I am at work." For this reason they tried all the more to kill him, because he not only broke the sabbath but he also called God his own father, making himself equal to God.

Jesus answered and said to them, "Amen, amen, I say to you, the Son cannot do anything on his own, but only what he sees the Father doing; for what he does, the Son will do also. For the Father loves the Son and shows him everything that he himself does, and he will show him greater works than these, so that you may be amazed. For just as the Father raises the dead and gives life, so also does the Son give life to whomever he wishes. Nor does the Father judge anyone, but he has given all judgment to the Son, so that all may honor the Son just as they honor the Father. Whoever does not honor the Son does not honor the Father who sent him. Amen, amen, I say to you, whoever hears my word and believes in the one who sent me has eternal life and will not come to condemnation, but has passed from death to life. Amen, amen, I say to you, the hour is coming and is now here when the dead will hear the voice of the Son of God, and those who hear will live. For just as the Father has life in himself, so also he gave to the Son the possession of life in himself. And he gave him power to exercise judgment, because he is the Son of Man. Do not be amazed at this, because the hour is coming in which all who are in the tombs will hear his voice and will come out, those who have done good deeds to the resurrection of life, but those who have done wicked deeds to the resurrection of condemnation.

"I cannot do anything on my own; I judge as I hear, and my judgment is just, because I do not seek my own will but the will of the one who sent me."

(1) *Light from light*

When we receive a great gift, we want to go to its source—my friend or my father, the giver—and express gratitude. What about the gift of Jesus himself? Where does he come from? Today Jesus opens to us the mystery of his heart. He has not come to speak about himself but to reveal the Father to us.

"My father is at work until now, so I am at work." Commenting on these words, Saint John says that for this reason the Jews are trying to kill Jesus. We may think the connection is exaggerated. They try to kill him because he speaks about the work of his father?

The Pharisees know well that Jesus is not speaking about Joseph of Nazareth or another person. When he says "my Father" he refers to the God Almighty. He pretends to be the Son of God, that is, he makes himself equal to God. And for that reason, he must die.

We can understand now the challenge of Jesus: the Jews can either follow him or deny him, but they cannot reduce as a mere pretension his claim to be one with God the Father. Christ speaks of himself as the Light that comes from the Light of the Father. As we say in the Creed, he is God from God and Light from Light, not just a mirror of the light of another, like the moon reflects the sun's brightness during the night. He is the light that comes from the Father, who sent him. "Whoever has seen me has seen the Father" (Jn 14:9).

If we want to follow Christ, we have to accept this challenge. To follow him implies to put our life at risk. Because "the light came into the world, but people preferred darkness to light" (Jn 3:19). And "whoever lives the truth comes to the light, so that his works may be clearly seen as done in God" (Jn 3:21).

(2) *The Father, the light to understand*

Without light we cannot see the world. As Light of the World, Christ gives us the key to understand the meaning of everything: the Father. We do not live in an empty world, nor do we live under the oppressive gaze of the big brother of Orwell's terrible novel, *1984*. The atmosphere of our existence is the tender presence of the Father. Like the sun, his eyes give us comfort, warmth, and serenity. We can apply the words of C. S. Lewis to this analogy: "I believe in Christianity as I believe that the sun has risen. Not only because I see it, but because by it I see everything else" (*Is Theology Poetry?*, 1945).

Think about the kid who is learning to ride the bicycle. His father is close to him, following his progress with his gaze. In a moment the father gets distracted with some thought and suddenly the kid falls to the ground. "Dad, you were not looking at me!" It is true. There is an invisible thread and a great power in our gaze and one that is unique in the eyes of a father. And we are the apple of his eyes!

With this revelation—God is Father—Jesus makes us able to grasp the meaning of our life. We are not some casual product of evolution but fruit of the love of God. As Benedict XVI put it, "each of us is willed, each of us is loved, each of us is necessary" (Beginning of the Petrine Ministry, Benedict XVI, April 24, 2005), as each of the children of a large family is unique and unrepeatable.

(3) *Light in our present: stained glasses*

We do not understand our lives without the light of the Father, revealed in Christ, his Son. But this light seems very far in time and space. How can we receive it? An example of Pope Francis will help us to understand it.

In the great gothic cathedrals "light comes down from heaven by passing through windows depicting the history of salvation. God's light comes to us through the account of his self-revelation and thus becomes capable of illuminating our passage through time" (*Lumen fidei*, 12). Between God's brightness and us, there is a great number of witnesses—stained glass windows—through which this light reaches us with many different colors.

We would prefer, perhaps to receive the light of God directly. The French philosopher Rousseau lamented once that he could not see God for himself: "How many people stand between God and me!" (see *Lumen fidei*, 14). From his individualistic conception, Rousseau could not understand the beauty of faith. The light of faith, the light of God, arrives to us through witnesses. This mediation implies that we can participate in the vision of another; we can share the knowledge with others!

How many people stand between God and me! Thank you, Lord, for all these witnesses, for these faces, this chain of light that has touched me and will continue after me.

For your prayer

The mystery of Jesus is the mystery of God the Father. Today I invite you to pray again with the Our Father. Be amazed before the name of God, revealed to us by Jesus: Father! Abbà! If Christ had not invited—and even commanded—us to do this, we would not dare to say this word!

Thursday (Fourth Week of Lent)

GOSPEL: JN 5:31–47

Jesus said to the Jews: "If I testify on my own behalf, my testimony cannot be verified. But there is another who testifies on my behalf, and I know that the testimony he gives on my behalf is true. You sent emissaries to John, and he testified to the truth. I do not accept testimony from a human being, but I say this so that you may be saved. He was a burning and shining lamp, and for a while you were content to rejoice in his light. But I have testimony greater than John's. The works that the Father gave me to accomplish, these works that I perform testify on my behalf that the Father has sent me. Moreover, the Father who sent me has testified on my behalf. But you have never heard his voice nor seen his form, and you do not have his word remaining in you, because you do not believe in the one whom he has sent. You search the Scriptures, because you think you have eternal life through them; even they testify on my behalf. But you do not want to come to me to have life.

"I do not accept human praise; moreover, I know that you do not have the love of God in you. I came in the name of my Father, but you do not accept me; yet if another comes in his own name, you will accept him. How can you believe, when you accept praise from one another and do not seek the praise that comes from the only God? Do not think that I will accuse you before the Father: the one who will accuse you is Moses, in whom you have placed your hope. For if you had believed Moses, you would have believed me, because he wrote about me. But if you do not believe his writings, how will you believe my words?"

(1) *The witnesses: lights of the Light*

The poet T. S. Eliot says that our sight is submarine. The fish in the ocean are able to see thanks to the light that comes from above. Likewise, in our life we see the light but we do not see the origin of this light.

Christ has come so that in him we may see the Father; in his light we see the origin of any light. And Christ has sent us witnesses, lights of his light. The brightness from heaven comes to us through the windows, through the stained glass of the witnesses. In this way this light receives colors and shapes; the white light is transformed into red, blue, yellow, and so many nuances. The hands of Jesus that touched the blind man's eyes and gave them vision are now the hands of our parents, siblings, spouse, children…

Today Jesus reminds us about the witnesses who testify on his behalf. He is not alone. First of all, John the Baptist, the "burning and shining lamp," points at him as the Lamb of God. Then the Scriptures, which record and keep the promises of God, offer their testimony. We also have the witness of Jesus' own life: the works and words he accomplishes. Finally, in all these signs, the Father who sent him testifies on his behalf.

God speaks to us through witnesses. They are not the origin, but they reveal it to us. This mediation is a sign of his humility and respect for our freedom. God could send daily fire and wonders from heaven but he wants to speak through ordinary witnesses in our daily life. He wants to have friends, not slaves.

Here we see the drama; Christ has many witnesses but the people do not want to come to him to have life. Jesus insists and insists but he will not force us to believe. Help us Lord to recognize your presence in these poor witnesses, workers in your vineyard: our spouses, our parents, our teachers, co-workers…

(2) *Moses, the accuser*

One of the witnesses to recognize Jesus is Moses. "I am not going to accuse you before the Father, but Moses accuses you." The mission of the witness is to proclaim the joy of Jesus. This task may imply in some moments to "accuse." To accuse is not to condemn or to judge, but to remind the others, to call to conversion, to try to awaken the hearts, as Jesus does today.

Why is Moses accusing us? During the covenant in the desert the people are to stay away from Mount Sinai and only Moses is able to speak with God. When Moses comes down from the mountain, the people see the radiant face of Moses and they cover it. But the glory of God is only visible through the illumination of Moses' face. The Israelites are called to believe in God from what Moses, a simple and tottering man, tells them.

With the coming of Jesus Christ we can see God face to face! Moses accuses the Jews, that is, calls them to conversion. They do not believe even though they can see now what the people of Israel were unable to see. And Moses accuses us: through the gift of the Holy Spirit and the sacraments you have the Son of God among you! Perhaps I can understand you do not believe in me, a weak and tottering Israelite, but he is the Son of God, the one who revealed himself in the burning bush and saved us from the Pharaoh.

Moses accuses us so that we may remember the great compassion of God in our lives. Remember his great promise and the blessings he has sent over you. Acknowledge the gift you have received.

(3) *Moses, the defender: the man of the breach*

As a witness, Moses accuses us; he reminds us of the mercy of God. But during his life, Moses was always the great defender of the people before God. As witness, he reveals God's will to the people and as intercessor, he speaks to God about his people.

Moses' whole life is an intercession for his people. We find him so many times reminding God of his mercy. The people have sinned and are far from God, following idols or complaining about the path in the desert. Then God speaks of exterminating them, but Moses, his chosen one asks him: Remember, God, your servants Abraham, Isaac and Israel, remember your promise. Do not destroy this people. Moses withstands God in the breach to turn back his destructive wrath (see Ps 106:19–20). He is the "man in the breach."

We find this mysterious person in other places of the Scripture:

> The people of the land practice extortion and commit

> robbery; they wrong the poor and the needy, and oppress the resident alien without justice. Thus I have searched among them for someone who would build a wall or stand in the breach before me to keep me from destroying the land; but I found no one. (Ez 22:29–31; see Is 59:14–16a)

God is looking for the man in the breach, who will stop his powerful hand. Perhaps we think that Moses calmed God who wanted to kill Israel. But this was not the case. God was looking for the man in the breach! He does not want to destroy his people but he wants to find someone—just one—who would pray for them. For that reason he is so pleased when Moses intercedes. We can imagine that God said to him: "Thank you! I thought nobody would come."

Moses, the man in the breach and defender of the people, is preparing the path of Jesus. In the fulfillment of time, God sends his own defender, his Son. Christ is the new Moses, the man in the breach. He has not come to accuse but to defend us: "Forgive them, Lord, they do not know..." He offers his life for us.

Finally, Christ sends his disciples as witnesses and intercessors. This mission is the vocation of the parents in the family and especially of the priests. The father and the mother intercede for their children. The priests, taken from among men and made their representative before God, offer their lives for all the faithful (see Heb 5:1).

For your prayer

Practice today the prayer of intercession. Think of the people the Lord has commended to you: your spouse, family, relatives, friends, your godson, your coworker, neighbors... And pray for them; ask Jesus to be merciful and to bless them with great gifts.

Consider in your prayer your vocation as witness and intercessor. You are called to speak about God wherever you are, as witness of his love. You are called to speak with God about your family and friends as a faithful intercessor.

Friday (Fourth Week of Lent)

GOSPEL: JN 7:1–2, 10, 25–30

Jesus moved about within Galilee; but he did not wish to travel in Judea, because the Jews were trying to kill him. But the Jewish feast of Tabernacles was near.

But when his brothers had gone up to the feast, he himself also went up, not openly but [as it were] in secret.

So some of the inhabitants of Jerusalem said, "Is he not the one they are trying to kill? And look, he is speaking openly and they say nothing to him. Could the authorities have realized that he is the Christ? But we know where he is from. When the Christ comes, no one will know where he is from." So Jesus cried out in the temple area as he was teaching and said, "You know me and also know where I am from. Yet I did not come on my own, but the one who sent me, whom you do not know, is true. I know him, because I am from him, and he sent me." So they tried to arrest him, but no one laid a hand upon him, because his hour had not yet come.

(1) *The great question: the origin*

Our Easter Vigil will begin with the sign of the fire. In the middle of the night, outside the church, the Easter Candle will be lit. It will be a sign of the complete victory of the light of Christ over darkness. Today, still walking through the desert, we see how the Jews try to arrest Jesus. We are getting closer to the mystery of our redemption and the war is already open.

Jesus has to come in secret to the feast and while he is speaking in the temple of Jerusalem they try to arrest him. This conflict is the fight between light and darkness. Today's first reading describes the meaning of this battle against Christ, the just. "He judges us debased; / . . . and boasts that God is his Father" (Ws 2:16). The Jews are blind and closed. They know not the hidden counsels of God.

"But we know where he is from." This is the great objection against Jesus. "He comes from Nazareth and we know his family." Again, the question is the origin of Jesus; who are you? Where do you come from? Who has sent you? Is your light like ours, a light that will fade and not endure?

Jesus answers with a very solemn proclamation. In the middle of the feast in the temple area, surrounded by a huge crowd, Jesus cries out: "You know me and you know where I am from." We can understand what he is telling them: You think you know me, you think you know where I am from. And he proclaims again the mystery of his origin: "Yet I did not come on my own, but the one who sent me, whom you do not know, is true." The Jews cannot accept Jesus because they do not know the Father, who has sent him. They are far from God, whom they should know through the Scriptures.

(2) *God's vocation, not just my decision*

What do we find in the origin of Jesus? A mission. The Father has sent him. It is not just his decision of coming to the earth but his vocation to be with us. Likewise, in the origin of our lives we do not find only our individualistic decision but the word of God calling us: Go! I need you!

If you are thinking what to do after high school or college, the right question is not just about my convenience, my desires, my future income. . . Have you asked the Lord, your creator? Because he is calling you and he needs you; he has a mission for you.

In the origin of your marriage, your family, and your work there is not just our human decision to get married or to receive these children. Otherwise later, in moments of difficulty you may think: "I chose the wrong husband" or "It was a great mistake." No. In the origin of your marriage and your parenthood there was not just your decision but your answer to God, who was calling you. Do not look for false consolation or self-pity thinking this was a mistake, but ask the Lord for his help to heal this relationship. He has promised to be with you all the days of your life.

We understand our lives better when we consider that in the origin of our lives there is a vocation, not just a decision. Of course later we will decide but this free act will always be our answer to God's call: yes or no, as acceptance or as rejection. In the origin of our identity there is Someone who has called us from nothing to existence. We are called by love and to love.

Of course, so often we are not aware of this call and this answer. We don't realize that in the origin of our existence and in the beginning of every day God is inviting us to a great friendship with him. It happens to us the same as Jacob experienced after his dream of the stairway reaching to the heavens. When he awoke from his sleep he said: "Truly, the LORD is in this place and I did not know it!" (Gn 28:16). Truly! The Lord is in your studies, in your marriage, in your time of discernment of a vocation, in every action of your daily life. Even if I did not know it, the Lord is in this place. Even in the times of struggles and wanderings, the Lord is there, calling, insisting, knocking at the door of your heart.

What if I say "No"? What if I reject his proposal? He will continue calling, trying to restore us to him. The call of God is irrevocable (see Rom 11:29). Respectful of our freedom, he will try again without losing hope. We can remember the story of Israel according to the prophet Hosea which is also our story. God is speaking, explaining his relationship with the people of Israel (where it says "Israel" or "Ephraim" you can read your name and your family).

> "When Israel was a child I loved him, / out of Egypt I called my son. / The more I called them, / the farther they went from me, / ... I drew them with human cords, / with bands of love; / I fostered them like those / who raise an infant to their cheeks; / I bent down to feed them / ... How could I give you up, Ephraim, / or deliver you up, Israel? / ... My heart is overwhelmed, / my pity is stirred. / I will not give vent to my blazing anger, / ... For I am God and not a man, / the Holy One present among you; / I will not come in wrath" (Hosea 11:1–2, 3, 4, 8).

(3) *The key point: the free gift of himself*

Therefore in the origin of Christ's life there is a vocation; the Father is sending him to us. Jesus is the "apostle" (the one who has been sent) of the Father. He has sent him to manifest the greatness of God's love. And Jesus knows that this revelation implies his death because the people love the darkness rather than the light (see Jn 3:19). Christ knows he is called to the gift of himself; his "hour" is coming.

The reference to the "hour" of Jesus is very important to the Gospel of Saint John. We find it for example at Cana, when Jesus explains to his mother that his hour has not yet come (see Jn 2:4). To the Samaritan woman, he says that "the hour is coming and is now here" in which we will worship the Father in Spirit and truth (see Jn 4:21–23). Today we know that "no one laid a hand upon him, because his hour had not yet come" (Jn 7:30). As we will see in Holy Week, the hour of Jesus is the time of his great love (see Jn 12:23; 13:1).

Jesus will die but not when his enemies want. We learn today there is an hour, a moment for the gift. The death of Christ will not be something that will happen but something accepted and chosen by him. He knows his hour is close and he will offer himself to the Father for our salvation.

For your prayer

Give thanks to the Lord because he comes to the cross freely: "This is why the Father loves me, because I lay down my life in order to take it up again. No one takes it from me, but I lay it down on my own. I have power to lay it down, and power to take it up again. This command I have received from my Father" (Jn 10:17–18).

Thank you, Lord, for your great generosity. Help me to join my sufferings and joys with you in my daily life. Help me to transform my life in a great Eucharist.

Saturday (Fourth Week of Lent)

GOSPEL: JN 7: 40–53

Some in the crowd who heard these words [of Jesus] said, "This is truly the Prophet." Others said, "This is the Christ." But others said, "The Christ will not come from Galilee, will he? Does not Scripture say that the Christ will be of David's family and come from Bethlehem, the village where David lived?" So a division occurred in the crowd because of him. Some of them even wanted to arrest him, but no one laid hands on him.

So the guards went to the chief priests and Pharisees, who asked them, "Why did you not bring him?" The guards answered, "Never before has anyone spoken like this one." So the Pharisees answered them, "Have you also been deceived? Have any of the authorities or the Pharisees believed in him? But this crowd, which does not know the law, is accursed." Nicodemus, one of their members who had come to him earlier, said to them, "Does our law condemn a man before it first hears him and finds out what he is doing?" They answered and said to him, "You are not from Galilee also, are you? Look and see that no prophet arises from Galilee." Then each went to his own house.

FROM ASH TO WATER

(1) *Innocence before the power of the light*

Only the little child was brave and innocent enough to say the truth: "The king is naked." As we read in the medieval Spanish tale of Don Juan Manuel, and later in Andersen, the king is deceived by two "fabulous weavers and tailors." They propose to the king to prepare marvelous new clothes for him. The special quality of these clothes consist in the fact that their special material is only visible for those with honest parents. In order to survey the progress of the clothes, the king sends two servants who, of course, can not see the material of the cloth but out of fear, they describe to the king the beauty of the new clothes. Finally, when the work is finished, the king wears the new clothes through the city. He is not able to see the costume. However, again out of fear and vanity, he praises its quality. Finally he wears these new clothes through the city and everybody remains silent, praising the new tailors, until one little child, the only innocent, humble, and brave, proclaims the truth: "The king is naked!"

Today's Gospel shows us innocence against vanity and prejudice. Those who hear Jesus with a pure heart are amazed at his wisdom and depth. The guards want to arrest Jesus but they do not lay their hands upon him. "Never before has anyone spoken like this man." They hear the words of the Master and, with innocent hearts, they are not able to bring him. Peter keeps in his heart the "words of eternal life" of Jesus (see Jn 6). How can we abandon you? Where will we go? The blind man conserves the same purity: "Never was it heard..." (see Jn 8).

Anyone with simplicity of heart experiences the power of the word of Jesus. The one who created heaven and earth with his word is now speaking in the temple. Who are you? When the people hear him, some of them are sure: "This is truly the Prophet. No doubt." Others, poisoned perhaps with the venom of the Pharisees, ask: "The Christ will not come from Galilee, will he?"

(2) *Choose your place: Pharisees, crowd, guards, or Nicodemus*

The time of Lent requires us to participate in the mystery. Nobody can be a pure observer, a passive attendant. We need to choose our place before Christ. Where are you? Perhaps you are with the Pharisees, with the crowd, the guards, or Nicodemus.

First of all we see the main agents in this Gospel: the chief priests and the Pharisees. They seem to be totally closed to Jesus. No matter what Jesus does, they have decided and closed their heart to his action. First they try to convince the people against Jesus. Later, when they see the division in the people, they proclaim: "This crowd is accursed." This outlook is the idea of totalitarianism; use the crowd as an object to your service and utility. Some days later the Pharisees will see the crowd welcoming Jesus to Jerusalem with olive branches and palms. Finally, before Pilate they will use the crowd to condemn Jesus.

Secondly, perhaps you belong to the crowd which is divided but seems to agree with Christ. As honest and simple men, the guards are really confused. They receive orders and they obey. But this time it is different. The command of the chief priests and Pharisees is impossible to accomplish. Hearing Jesus, their hearts are burning. "Never before has anyone spoken like this man." But at the end, the crowd is a crowd; it is not active and intelligent, but passive, docile to the guidance of others. If you choose the crowd prepare yourself to be guided and to lose your identity in the anonymity of the people.

Thirdly, we find Nicodemus. He is a Pharisee—not the only one—who has believed in Jesus. He risks his life and his future for Christ. "Does our law condemn a man before it first hears him and finds out what he is doing?" Finally we see courageous friends of Jesus!

Do not go against the light. You are not called to remain in the crowd. Follow Nicodemus and risk your life for Jesus. Like the little child in the tale of the new clothes of the king, do not be afraid of the truth. Remember Blessed John Henry Newman and his path toward Catholicism. He gave thanks to the Lord because with his grace "he had not sinned against the light."

(3) *To you I have entrusted my cause!*

Choose your place from which you will contemplate Jesus. You can remember that from the beginning of the Gospel but especially from now on, the true agent of this story is Christ himself. The Pharisees will plan so many plots against him: "Let us destroy the tree in its vigor" (Jer 11:19). But Jesus is aware of all this. Nothing escapes his hand and wisdom: "I knew their plot because the Lord informed me; at that time you, O Lord, showed me their doings" (see Jer 11:18–20). Again we see that it is not the time, the "hour" of Jesus. He will go to the Passion "like a trusting lamb led to slaughter," offering himself freely to the Father.

The prophet Jeremiah helps us to understand the prayer of Jesus in these days. As Jeremiah, so Jesus knows the end is close and he is growing in his trust in the Lord. His life is, like always, under the eyes of the Father. Into his hands he commends his whole being. "But you, LORD of hosts, just Judge, / searcher of mind and heart, / ...to you I have entrusted my cause!" (Jer 11:20).

For your prayer

Choose your place before the Lord. Consider the position of the Pharisees, the crowd, the guards, Nicodemus. Will you risk your life for Jesus?

LAZARUS: OUR FRIEND

(FIFTH WEEK OF LENT)

Fifth Sunday of Lent (A)

GOSPEL: JN 11:1–45

Now a man was ill, Lazarus from Bethany, the village of Mary and her sister Martha. Mary was the one who had anointed the Lord with perfumed oil and dried his feet with her hair; it was her brother Lazarus who was ill. So the sisters sent word to him saying, "Master, the one you love is ill." When Jesus heard this he said, "This illness is not to end in death, but is for the glory of God, that the Son of God may be glorified through it." Now Jesus loved Martha and her sister and Lazarus. So when he heard that he was ill, he remained for two days in the place where he was. Then after this he said to his disciples, "Let us go back to Judea." The disciples said to him, "Rabbi, the Jews were just trying to stone you, and you want to go back there?" Jesus answered, "Are there not twelve hours in a day? If one walks during the day, he does not stumble, because he sees the light of this world. But if one walks at night, he stumbles, because the light is not in him." He said this, and then told them, "Our friend Lazarus is asleep, but I am going to awaken him." So the disciples said to him, "Master, if he is asleep, he will be saved." But Jesus was talking about his death, while they thought that he meant ordinary sleep. So then Jesus said to them clearly, "Lazarus has died. And I am glad for you that I was not there, that you may believe. Let us go to him." So Thomas, called Didymus, said to his fellow disciples, "Let us also go to die with him."

When Jesus arrived, he found that Lazarus had already been in the tomb for four days. Now Bethany was near Jerusalem, only about two miles away. And many of the Jews had come to Martha and Mary to comfort them about their brother. When Martha heard that Jesus was coming, she went to meet him; but Mary sat at home. Martha said to Jesus, "Lord, if you had been here, my brother would not have died. But even now I know that whatever you ask of God, God will give you." Jesus said to her, "Your brother will rise." Martha said to him, "I know he will rise, in the resurrection on the last day." Jesus told her, "I am the resurrection and the life; whoever believes in me, even if he dies, will live, and everyone who lives and believes in me will never die. Do you believe this?" She said to him, "Yes, Lord. I have come to believe that you are the Christ, the Son of God, the one who is coming into the world."

When she had said this, she went and called her sister Mary secretly, saying, "The teacher is here and is asking for you." As soon as she heard this, she rose quickly and went to him. For Jesus had not yet come into the village, but was still where Martha had met him. So when the Jews who were with her in the house comforting her saw Mary get up quickly and go out, they followed her, presuming that she was going to the tomb to weep there. When Mary came to where Jesus was and saw him, she fell at his feet and said to him, "Lord, if you had been here, my brother would not have died." When Jesus saw her weeping and the Jews who had come with her weeping, he became perturbed and deeply troubled, and said, "Where have you laid him?" They said to him, "Sir, come and see." And Jesus wept. So the Jews said, "See how he loved him." But some of them said, "Could not the one who opened the eyes of the blind man have done something so that this man would not have died?"

So Jesus, perturbed again, came to the tomb. It was a cave, and a stone lay across it. Jesus said, "Take away the stone." Martha, the dead man's sister, said to him, "Lord, by now there will be a stench; he has been dead for four days." Jesus said to her, "Did I not tell you that if you believe you will see the glory of God?" So they took away the stone. And Jesus raised his eyes and said, "Father, I thank you for hearing me. I know that you always hear me; but because of the crowd here I have said this, that they may believe that you sent me." And when he had said this, He cried out in a loud voice, "Lazarus, come out!" The dead man came out, tied hand and foot with burial bands, and his face was wrapped in a cloth. So Jesus said to them, "Untie him and let him go."

Now many of the Jews who had come to Mary and seen what he had done began to believe in him.

(1) *"The one you love": my definition*

We are in the last week before Palm Sunday and Holy Week. These days can be our "final sprint" in our Lent, days of special grace and prayer. Remember what Saint Ignatius of Loyola used to say: "One intense action is far more worthy than a thousand lukewarm. What a lazy man cannot accomplish in many years, an energetic man usually achieves in a short time" (Letter to the Students of Coimbra, May 1547). If we have been tepid in this Lent we still have time to begin again like Lazarus, who, hearing Jesus' voice, began a new life. In a short time we can make great progress in our knowledge of the heart of Christ.

After the meeting of the Samaritan woman and the blind man with Christ, today we consider the life of the family of Bethany with Lazarus, Martha, and Mary. If Jesus was water for the thirsty woman and light for the blind young man, today he reveals himself as the powerful friend who is able to overcome death with only his word. And today, as in the other weeks, we also see that the joy of this encounter is for our family. The Samaritan's family, her children, were in really bad shape after five husbands. The blind man's family, his parents, were afraid of the Jews and were not able to risk their lives for Christ. Today, Lazarus' family, his sisters, are also destroyed because of grief and pain. Their brother is dead and Jesus, supposedly their friend, has done nothing in order to help him.

It seems that Lazarus was a good friend of Jesus. Close to Jerusalem, his house was like Jesus' headquarters: a perfect place to rest, reflect, and plan after a busy and harsh day of discussions with the Pharisees. In the Gospels we find several moments in which Jesus is having dinner with this family. Now, Lazarus is really sick and Martha and Mary decide to send Jesus a message. "Master, the one you love is ill." They thought this statement would be enough for Jesus to understand the situation. It is not necessary to add anything else: "The one you love." Jesus would understand.

In fact, Jesus does understand. Without a special master's degree in anthropology or theology, these two sisters offer to us in four words a complete definition of the human being, of ourselves. Who am I? Like Lazarus, Martha, and Mary, I am "the one Jesus loves." I am also sick and a sinner, but first of all, I am "the one he loves."

But Jesus comes late. His friend is suffering and dying and he continues his journey! What kind of friend is Jesus? Why is he so late? Sometimes we arrive late to our appointments. The reasons are very different, sometimes because of an unexpected emergency, other times because—perhaps without realizing—we think that our time is more important and precious than our friends. Jesus' delay is not due to a lack of organization or wisdom. He knows he is late but he also knows that this illness is not to end in death but is for the glory of God. Through Lazarus the Son of God will be glorified and the disciples will believe in him.

Lord, why do you come late? Why don't you help us right now and here? Why don't you reveal your great love to my sister, who is suffering so much? Why don't you heal my son from his slavery? Jesus has a project, a plan. He is not coming late but in the right moment so that we may rejoice and believe in him.

(2) *"The one you have created for the resurrection"*

When Jesus arrives, Lazarus has been several days in the tomb.

After his dialogue with Martha and Mary, Jesus goes to the tomb and weeps before his dead friend. "See how he loved him!" See how he loves you! Jesus cries when he sees the tomb of my sin and my death. If I am "the one he loves," he is "the one who has wept for me."

But Jesus is not just one friend more among the others. He is also "the one who opened the eyes of the blind." The people ask: Could not he have done something else, other than crying? Jesus does do something else.

"Take away the stone." Like in Cana of Galilee and in so many other places, Jesus will need our help in order to work the miracle. He needs our water, our five loaves and two fish, our effort to take away the stone. Finally when everything is prepared, he prays and reveals again the secret of his life: "Father, I thank you for hearing me." Only after this does Jesus cry out in a loud voice: "Lazarus, come out!" The Father gives to his human voice an incredible power. These three words come to the place of the dead and awaken Lazarus to new life.

Imagine the surprise of the crowd and of Martha and Mary when they saw Lazarus coming out of the tomb, tied hand and foot with burial bands and probably with a stench. Again Jesus needs our help: "Untie him and let him go." Imagine you are one of Lazarus' friends or one of his servants. With your own hands you untie the bands and you testify to the power of Jesus' voice.

Who is Lazarus? He is not just "the one who Jesus loves," but also someone called to the resurrection. He has not been created just to die but to overcome the barrier of death and live eternally. Lazarus is a living sign of Jesus' power. The promise of Ezekiel (see Ez 37:12–14) has been accomplished in him. God opens the tombs of the people and brings them back to their land. Before Jesus, death is like a dream!

Today we are called, with Mary and Martha, to fortify our faith and hope in eternal life. "I am the resurrection and the life.... Do you believe this?" (Jn 11: 25–26). Martha invites us today to place all of our hope in our friend: "Yes, Lord, I believe that you are the Messiah, the Son of God, the one who is coming into this world" (Jn 11:27). Death is not the meaning of our existence. God has created us in Christ for resurrection and life. This truth gives an authentic and definitive meaning to everything. Our belief in eternal life impacts our vision of history, our culture and politics, and of course, the economy (see Benedict XVI, Message for Lent 2011). When we understand that our definitive resurrection is the purpose of the whole world and the purpose of our life, we can look in a different way at our spouse and children. My work, my daily life, the way I educate my children, the way I clean every day this room, the way I speak with my parents… All these have a different "color" with the light of the resurrection. In these small and daily actions eternity is at stake! They are our baby steps toward resurrection and life. Otherwise everything would finish shut within a tomb devoid of any hope.

(3) *"The one who will die with you"*

But Lazarus is not yet in heaven. He will die again. He lives between two deaths, or better, between two resurrections: the first one through the word of Jesus, Come out!, and the second and definitive one at the end of time. Imagine the first days of his new life. Everything now has a special taste, a special light. After his being in the tomb, he has a new way of looking, touching, smelling, tasting, hearing, speaking, thinking…

Can we imagine Lazarus' new life? We also live between two deaths and two resurrections. Lazarus' resurrection is for us a sign of our baptism. We were also in the tomb and Jesus cried in a loud voice: "Come out!" The waters of baptism have given us a new life: a new way of touching, smelling, tasting, watching, loving…

A few days later Lazarus receives a message: "The one you love is sick, he has been condemned to death. The one you love is dying on the cross." Jesus gives Lazarus—and us—a new definition: You are the one for the sake of whom Jesus offers his life, his body and blood.

We know the Pharisees decide Lazarus should also die. He is a sign of the power of Jesus; simply his presence at work or at a dinner is able to make many disciples of Jesus. The people go to Bethany to see him and they follow Jesus.

You may think about your life. From the day of your baptism, you live a new life, like that of Lazarus after his resurrection. Simply your presence is called to make many disciples of Jesus. How do people "see" this power of Jesus in your life? In your daily love and forgiveness with your spouse, in the many tasks at home and with your children, in your conversations with your friends and co-workers, how do they recognize the incredible power of Christ? Become a witness of his love. For sure, this demonstration will imply struggles and even persecution. Do not worry. Do not be afraid. Just remember in whom you have believed: he is able to guard you (see 2 Tim 1:12).

We don't know if the Pharisees really accomplished their threat. In any case, their evil decision to kill Lazarus helps us to understand that Lazarus—and we with him—is one called to be wherever Christ is. He is a sign of Jesus' power; he will die and rise with him. He is the friend of Christ: "the one you love."

For your prayer

Insist today on the act of the presence of God, at the beginning of your prayer. You can use the words of Martha:

"Lord, I know that whatever you ask of God, God will give you."

"Lord. I have come to believe that you are the Christ, the Son of God, the one who is coming into the world."

WE WOULD LIKE TO SEE JESUS: OUR FRIEND

(FIFTH WEEK OF LENT)

Fifth Sunday of Lent (B)

GOSPEL: JN 12:20–33

Some Greeks who had come to worship at the Passover Feast-Now among those who went up to worship at the feast were some Greeks. So these came to Philip, who was from Bethsaida in Galilee, and asked him, "Sir, we would like to see Jesus." Philip went and told Andrew; then Andrew and Philip went and told Jesus. Jesus answered them, "The hour has come for the Son of Man to be glorified. Amen, amen, I say to you, unless a grain of wheat falls to the ground and dies, it remains just a grain of wheat; but if it dies, it produces much fruit. Whoever loves his life loses it, and whoever hates his life in this world will preserve it for eternal life. Whoever serves me must follow me, and where I am, there also will my servant be. The Father will honor whoever serves me.

"I am troubled now. Yet what should I say? 'Father, save me from this hour'? But it was for this purpose that I came to this hour. Father, glorify your name." Then a voice came from heaven, "I have glorified it and will glorify it again." The crowd there heard it and said it was thunder; but others said, "An angel has spoken to him." Jesus answered and said, "This voice did not come for my sake but for yours. Now is the time of judgment on this world; now the ruler of this world will be driven out. And when I am lifted up from the earth, I will draw everyone to myself." He said this indicating the kind of death he would die.

Meditations for Lent

(1) *All the nations shall come to adore him*

We are very close to the holy week, very close to the mystery of our salvation. Today's gospel prepares our heart for the "hour" of Jesus, the time of his offering and death. Saint John describes us the tension of the days before the Last Supper and the passion of Jesus.

After the resurrection of Lazarus, the Jews had made the decision to kill Jesus. Then, just six days before Passover, Jesus was anointed in Bethany and he spoke about his death: "Let her keep this for the day of my burial." Jesus knows his hour is coming, he knows about the plots of the Jews, but he knows he is called to proclaim the great love of God the Father, even unto death.

In this atmosphere of preparation for Easter, some Greeks have come to Jerusalem and they want to see Jesus. Two apostles will bring the message to the Lord. *Philip* and *Andrew* are Greek names. We know these apostles come from Galilee and probably they were familiar with the Greek.

"Sir, we would like to see Jesus." When the Lord receives this message, something very strange happens. We may think Jesus is a little bit confused by the way he answers. They tell him that some Greeks want to see him and he replies mentioning the hour of the Son of man and the grain of wheat that falls to the ground. This kind of strange answers of Jesus are very common in the gospel of Saint John.

In the desire of the Greeks to see him, Jesus discovers something very important. These people want to *see* him. For Saint John, seeing and believing are very close. Like John, who "saw and believed" (Jn 20:8), these Greeks want to see Jesus—they want to believe in him.

Why is so special that some Greeks will believe in Jesus? In the prophet Isaiah we read that God makes a promise: "I am coming to gather all nations and tongues; they shall come and see my glory" (Is 66:18). God "gathers the dispersed of Israel" (Is 56:8). "Nations shall walk by your light…the riches of the sea shall be poured out before you, the wealth of nations shall come to you" (Is 60:3.5).

When Jesus hears that the Greeks want to see him and believe in him, he realizes that God is accomplishing his promise. Therefore, his Hour is close.

We ask today to the Lord that we may become like Philip and Andrew, messengers between Jesus and those who want to see them. We may think in our children and grandchildren, our spouse, relatives, friends... They may come to us with questions or with the desire of knowing more about Jesus and his Church. There is an apostle present in us. Be welcoming, be prepared to guide these "Greeks" to Jesus!

(2) *The law of the grain of wheat*

The Hour of Jesus has been patiently prepared. Now it is the time of his "suffering transformation." Jesus compares himself with a grain of wheat. Unless this grain falls to the ground and dies, it remains just a grain of wheat. Jesus doesn't want to remain just what he is. He wants to be fruitful in us, he wants to bring us eternal life offering his temporal life.

Do you want to remain what you are? Jesus is guiding us in the path of fruitfulness. We are not called to preserve our lives but to offer them. This will imply to go out of our comfort-zone and accept suffering.

Jesus comes as the grain of wheat that will die and produce much fruit. By his death he will give us new life. This is what we experience in each Mass. As Benedict XVI puts it, "this grain of wheat falls into the earth and thus the new Bread grows, the Bread of future life, the Blessed Eucharist that nourishes us and is open to the divine mysteries for new life" (Benedict XVI, 25 July 2005).

We don't want to remain as we are. In our heart we find the desire of being fruitful. Jesus gives us today the law of the fruit: we need to accept this suffering transformation so that the fruit mature and may be sweet nourishment to others. Our patient silences, our forgiveness, our "let it go"...will fructify in our family life.

(3) *"I am troubled now"*

Today Jesus is troubled. Thinking in his future suffering and death, he is anxious and troubled. "What should I say? Should I avoid the suffering." It is consoling for us to see that Jesus is so close to us. Like us, he feels anxiety and fear, he trembles and cries. The one whose word worked so many wonders is now afraid and troubled.

Jesus wants to be with us in our sufferings. He wants to help us to understand the meaning of each of our struggles. "It was for this purpose that I came to this hour. Father, glorify your name." There is a purpose in our suffering. Whenever we suffer physically or spiritually, we can find Jesus at our side and we can offer everything with him. When our "Hour" arrives, we can be close to the Lord and glorify the name of God, my Father.

For your prayer

In times of distress and suffering, we can pray with Jesus Psalm 23, remembering God is our shepherd.

"The Lord is my shepherd; there is nothing I lack. In green pastures he makes me lie down; to still waters he leads me; he restores my soul. He guides me along right paths for the sake of his name. Even though I walk through the valley of the shadow of death, I will fear no evil, for you are with me; your rod and your staff comfort me. You set a table before me in front of my enemies; You anoint my head with oil; my cup overflows. Indeed, goodness and mercy will pursue me all the days of my life; I will dwell in the house of the Lord for endless days."

NEITHER DO I CONDEMN YOU: OUR FRIEND

(FIFTH WEEK OF LENT)

Fifth Sunday of Lent (*C*)

GOSPEL: JN 8:1–11

Jesus went to the Mount of Olives. But early in the morning he arrived again in the temple area, and all the people started coming to him, and he sat down and taught them. Then the scribes and the Pharisees brought a woman who had been caught in adultery and made her stand in the middle. They said to him, "Teacher, this woman was caught in the very act of committing adultery. Now in the law, Moses commanded us to stone such women. So what do you say?" They said this to test him, so that they could have some charge to bring against him. Jesus bent down and began to write on the ground with his finger. But when they continued asking him, he straightened up and said to them,[c] "Let the one among you who is without sin be the first to throw a stone at her." Again he bent down and wrote on the ground. And in response, they went away one by one, beginning with the elders. So he was left alone with the woman before him. Then Jesus straightened up and said to her, "Woman, where are they? Has no one condemned you?" She replied, "No one, sir." Then Jesus said, "Neither do I condemn you. Go, [and] from now on do not sin any more."

(1) *Life himself encounters the culture of death*

Who will die? The scribes and Pharisees have decided that someone will die today. They have caught a woman in adultery and therefore she must die. But then they have a better idea: "let us ask Jesus and test him. If he agrees, the woman will die and he will need to stop speaking about mercy and forgiveness. The people will understand he was just a liar. If he disagrees and wants to save the woman, we will stone him, because he speaks against the law of Moses."

Who will die today? The scene is full with drama, or better, with tragedy. The life of this woman depends on Jesus. But also the life of the Lord is in danger. If he agrees with killing the woman, then he will betray his vocation and he will have "died" as prophet of mercy. If he rejects the law, they will denounce him and kill him (and the adulterer with him).

These are the thoughts of the culture of death. Someone needs to die. There is no hope for the adulterer neither for Jesus. Applying this to our time, we could say, that if as a result of adultery a baby has been conceived, he should also die. Dealing with abortion and other issues, Saint John Paul II spoke about about the culture of death in his encyclical *Evangelium Vitae* (*The Gospel of Life*, 12). A culture of death is a structure of sin which denies solidarity and is a war of the powerful against the weak, a conspiracy against life.

What will Jesus say? Jesus loves silence. He doesn't hurry. He knows that, according to the Scripture, "God did not make death, and he does not delight in the death of the living" (Wis 1:13). Jesus doesn't answer immediately, but he begins to write on the ground with his finger. We can imagine he is sad because of the adulterer's sin and because of the Pharisees hatred. He is also angry because of the hardness of heart of the scribes. So during this brief time he prays to the Father.

But the scribes and Pharisees want an answer. They continue asking Jesus until he straightens up and answers: "Let the one among you who is without sin be the first to throw a stone at her." What a wonderful reply! He should be grateful to the Jews for their stubbornness, since they gave us such a wonderful answer from Jesus. In these words, we can find an antidote against our complains, judgments, sadness, anger...

"Let the one among you who is without sin be the first to throw a stone at her." With this answer Jesus saves the life of this woman. Only two persons could throw a stone: He and his mother, Mary. And, because they are without sin, they will never do such thing.

After his response, Jesus again bends down and writes on the ground. He gives the Jews time to receive his words and act properly. In this case, they will accept his teaching. They cannot do otherwise. Beginning with the elders, they go away one by one. Jesus has spoken to the heart of each of them. He has placed before them the misery and poverty of their lives, and at least this time, they leave the scene in silence.

What was Jesus writing on the ground? Some authors think that he was writing the sins of the Jews and scribes, reminding them their weaknesses. As they saw them written on the ground they left, one by one. Saint Augustine thinks that this gesture portrays Christ as God, the divine legislator. As God wrote the law with his finger on tablets of stone and gave it to Moses, now Jesus is the Legislator, the Justice in person (cf. *Commentary on John's Gospel,* 33,5). He writes on the ground the new law of forgiveness. He, Life himself, overcomes the culture of death.

(2) *The transforming power of forgiveness*

In the island of Martha's Vineyard, located south of Cape Cod (Massachusetts), there is a chapel dedicated to Saint Augustine and with very nice stain glass windows. One of the windows depicts the sacrament of confession and says: "Go and sin no more." During the summer, without air conditioned, they usually open all the windows. The pane of the window which is opened is the one with the "no." As a result, when you enter the chapel you look at the stain glass which says: Go and sin…more!"

We know Jesus was eating and drinking with sinners—Pharisees, tax-collectors…and he even called some of them to be his disciples. But Jesus' approach to the people is always a challenge and a call to go out of the comfort-zone. He never said to anyone: "You have sinned, but don't worry. Remain where you are right now." When he speaks to the adulterer, we find the same pattern. He doesn't tell the woman: "It is ok, don't worry, you betrayed your spouse, it's not that bad. Take it easy."

Salvation comes through forgiveness, not through forgetfulness or ignorance. Jesus saves the woman by forgiving her and calling her to conversion. "Go, and from now on do not sin any more." Jesus puts her before her sin: "You have sinned, and your sin is destroying you and your family. But I come to save you. I don't condemn you but I want to transform your heart."

Can we even imagine the gratitude of this adulterer toward Jesus? We are unable to perceive the deep and amazing transformation that happened in the heart of this woman. Real forgiveness transformed her. This was the justice that also saved Saul of Tarsus, transforming him into St. Paul. This is the justice that will transform us and our family.

(3) *A good confession before (or during) Holy Week*

A few years ago, around the *Roe vs. Wade* sad anniversary, there was a beautiful homily at our parish regarding the culture of life. The main point of the preaching was the following: Abortion will end when the women who have had and suffered it, will stand up and make their voices heard. The best apostles of a culture of life are the mothers who had an abortion and later understood their great mistake and sin. Many of them now recognize how this action destroyed their life and how the mercy of God rebuilt their lives, their marriage, their hope...

Confession transforms us. We were sinners and through the mercy of God we have been reconciled with him. As a sacrament of reconciliation, a banquet of forgiveness, a reminder of God's mercy...confession is called to be a feast of joy.

However, many times we look at confession with something between fear and apprehension. Why are you afraid? Going to church, making the line of the sinners, telling my faults to a priest, recognizing this sin… We always find good excuses to postpone one day more the time of confession. It will be always "next week."

In this last week of Lent, I invite you to come to confession. Do not be afraid. When I recognize my sin, I also recognize the amazing mercy of the Father. I have sinned, but his love endures forever. I have sinned, but his mercy is always greater than any of my faults.

Confession is always a great blessing. It helps us to look at our life with the eyes of God. Confession is not just a point of arrival, but a point of departure. It is not just the moment in which I clean my heart throwing away my sin. It is the opportunity of a new beginning, of new strength. As saint Paul puts it:

"One thing I do, forgetting what lies behind and straining forward to what lies ahead. I press on toward the goal for the prize of the upward call of God in Christ Jesus" (Phil 3: 13–14).

For your prayer

Prepare a good confession by doing a nice examination of your heart.

Monday (Fifth Week of Lent)

GOSPEL: JN 8:1–11

Jesus went to the Mount of Olives. But early in the morning he arrived again in the temple area, and all the people started coming to him, and he sat down and taught them. Then the scribes and the Pharisees brought a woman who had been caught in adultery and made her stand in the middle. They said to him, "Teacher, this woman was caught in the very act of committing adultery. Now in the law, Moses commanded us to stone such women. So what do you say?" They said this to test him, so that they could have some charge to bring against him. Jesus bent down and began to write on the ground with his finger. But when they continued asking him, he straightened up and said to them, "Let the one among you who is without sin be the first to throw a stone at her." Again he bent down and wrote on the ground. And in response, they went away one by one, beginning with the elders. So he was left alone with the woman before him. Then Jesus straightened up and said to her, "Woman, where are they? Has no one condemned you?" She replied, "No one, sir." Then Jesus said, "Neither do I condemn you. Go, [and] from now on do not sin any more."

(1) *"The one who has sinned": justice or mercy?*

Yesterday we considered Lazarus' new life. His resurrection helps us to understand the new existence we began to enjoy the day of our baptism. Today we consider another "resurrection" performed by Jesus. Lazarus came back to life when he was already dead. Today we see him saving a woman caught in adultery. In this case it is not exactly a resurrection like Lazarus,' since Jesus works before the death of the woman. But it really is the resurrection of this woman, dead by her great sin.

Jesus comes from the Mount of Olives where he has spent long hours of the night praying to the Father. After this time together with God, the origin of the Law and perfect in mercy, he comes to the temple of Jerusalem. Then the scribes and Pharisees come with this poor woman.

Saint Augustine says that in this moment we hear two different voices: the "voice of justice" (scribes and Pharisees) and the "voice of mercy" (Jesus). The enemies of Jesus come with the power of the law: According to Moses, she has to die. What do you say, teacher? Of course, the Pharisees do not care about the woman and, in this moment, they do not care either for the law; they want to test Jesus and have some charge against him. They want to kill Jesus and the woman, the just and the sinner together. If he says this...we will condemn him. If he says that...we will condemn him. There seems to be no exit.

What is Jesus' answer, the "voice of mercy"? Of course, Jesus does not say: "Let her be stoned" since he has not come to condemn but to save and offer his life for the sinners. But neither does he say: "Do not throw a stone at her" since he is not against the law. With his voice of mercy, Jesus is not against the voice of justice. On the contrary, his mercy fulfills every justice, brings about a new justice.

What is his answer? Jesus begins to write on the ground with his finger. When they insist, he straightens up and says to them, "Let the one among you who is without sin be the first to throw a stone at her." And he continues writing on the ground.

Jesus brings a greater justice! In common usage "justice" implies "to render to every man his due." This interpretation was the definition given by Ulpian, a famous Roman jurist of the third century. If I have worked forty hours a week during one month, it is "due" to me this particular income. If I have paid this bill, it is "due" to me this particular service at home. This woman is caught in adultery; she must die. But is this law really just?

What do we choose, justice or mercy? Today's Gospel reveals to us that the justice of God has been manifested through faith in Jesus Christ (see Rom 3:21–22). Jesus brings divine justice. He is not rendering to every man his "due." His justice consists in this: the just man dies for the guilty and the guilty receives in return the blessing "due" to the just one. The woman caught in adultery does not die, but is forgiven. What kind of justice is this? Perhaps each one receives the contrary of his "due"? (see Benedict XVI, Message for Lent 2010).

The justice of the Cross teaches us how we are not self-made persons. We are in need of Another in order to realize ourselves fully.

This new justice invites us to exit the illusion of self-sufficiency. We need the others and God; we need his forgiveness and his friendship. Perhaps we rebel before this justice because we don't like to depend on others. Humility is required to accept that I need another to free me from what is mine—my sin—and to give me gratuitously what is God's: his forgiveness and life.

Justice and mercy. With Christ's love and compassion, a new justice has come. With the victory of Christ's mercy we enter into the "greatest" justice which is that of love (see Rom 13:8–10). Of course, with this new justice, Jesus is not fostering sin. "Sin no more!" Jesus does not tell the woman: "Neither do I condemn you. Go and continue living your same life. Be sure of my absolution. No matter what you sin, I will free you from any punishment" (Commentary to the Gospel of St. John, ch 33, 6). Jesus is not condemning nor praising. He calls her to conversion, to sin no more: Go, come back to your home, forgive, and ask for forgiveness. Do not wait until tomorrow or later. It has to be now: "Go and sin no more."

Like the adulterous woman, we can understand the meaning of the new life brought by Christ to our life. I am the one who has sinned and—through the greatest love of Jesus, without deserving it—I have been forgiven!

(2) *"The (only) one who is free from sin": do not judge*

"Let the one among you who is without sin be the first to throw a stone at her." Only Jesus and Mary would have been able to throw a stone at her. And of course they do not. We can imagine Jesus is telling the Pharisees: "Ok. You can stone her. The only condition is that you are without sin. Ok. You can judge her and condemn her. I only ask you to be sure you are without sin."

Then, instead of throwing the stone, Jesus begins to write on the ground with his finger. Saint Augustine asks about this mysterious action of Jesus. Why is he writing? What is he writing with his finger?

"The finger of God," he answers, "wrote the law, but because they were hard of heart, the law was written on stone. Now, the Lord writes on sand because he is looking for fruit" (*Commentary to the Gospel of St. John*, ch 33, 5).

Jesus is waiting for fruit: fruits of humility and conversion in the Pharisees and in the woman. He waits until the Pharisees understand they are sinners and therefore they cannot judge, condemn, and stone the sinner. John says they all went away one by one, beginning with the elders. Perhaps the elders began to leave because they were greater sinners? More likely because as elder, they are aware of their weakness and they are able to recognize quickly their sin.

Who am I to judge? Jesus, the creator of heaven and earth, the judge of everything, says: "Neither do I condemn you." We know this does not mean that it is ok what you have done. It does mean: "I do not condemn you but I save you. You can go, but from now on do not sin any more. I have saved your life from stoning, in order to save your heart from the greater slavery of sin and adultery."

Who am I to judge my spouse, my parents, my in-laws, my neighbors, my boss, or even my children? Complaining, gossiping, making judgments. . .all these are different ways of stoning with my heart. This rejection of judging does not mean, of course, to ignore or to justify the sin. If I see the sins of my beloved, I am called to pray for them and to help them. And if their sin is harmful to others, I am called to act against that, patiently and thoughtfully. In any case, complaining and gossiping are always useless solutions. I do not know any husband or wife who was changed by the complaints or judgments of the spouse. I know instead beautiful witnesses of spouses transformed through the forgiveness, prayer, and intelligent love of their spouses.

We can think that the new justice of Christ is the justice of the prophet who is the one who sees God's plan, the one who sees the future. Jesus forgives this woman because he is able to see a future of faithfulness for her. "Neither do I condemn you." I see your future and I know you are greater than what you have done. There is hope for you!

(3) *Keep Your Place: Do Not Desert*

Adultery is a sin against the unity of marriage; I will love you forever, I will love only you. In the Old Testament, God reveals himself as the faithful husband that loves and forgives again and again the unfaithful wife. Adultery is an image of any other sin. It begins with boredom in our love and with the temptation of looking other places, at other persons outside of my vocation. I experience anxiety and stress and I want to go away from our place, looking for better opportunities.

We understand the temptation of adultery if we look at the Benedictine monks. In their vows, they include a vote of stability. They promise to stay, as far as possible, in the same monastery in which they begin their path. They are not called to travel from one country to another but to remain in the same place, with the same walls and persons. The reason is only one; this monastery is the place where God spoke to them and revealed his glory and mission. Even if now he is silent, they know he will speak again in that place.

The vote of stability of the Benedictine monk helps us to understand the mystery of marriage. The spouses do not make this vote; on the contrary, they usually move several times for different reasons and their family life is full of unexpected movements, visits to the doctor, travels to see the family… But the spouses promise fidelity to each other forever. They understand this place—the heart of my spouse—is the place where God has spoken and revealed his glory and mission. Perhaps now, during this year of marriage, God remains silent, but we know he will speak again in this very same place.

Keep your place. Do not desert. If in your heart you experience boredom or anxiety, come back to the Lord. Encounter his mercy in the confessional. Ask him to reveal to you his glory in the daily life of your marriage and family.

For your prayer

Today you can remember the impactful story of the adulterous woman of Ezekiel 16. Pray also with Saint Augustine's final conversion to the Lord (*Confessions*, book VIII):

And you, O Lord, how long? How long, Lord, will you be angry for ever? Remember not our former iniquities, for I felt that I was held by them. I sent up these sorrowful words: How long, how long, "tomorrow, and tomorrow?" Why not now? Why not is there this hour an end to my uncleanness?

So was I speaking and weeping in the most bitter contrition of my heart, when, lo! I heard from a neighboring house a voice, as of boy or girl, I know not, chanting, and oft repeating, "Take up and read; Take up and read." Instantly, my countenance altered, I began to think most intently whether children were wont in any kind of play to sing such words: nor could I remember ever to have heard the like. So checking the torrent of my tears, I arose; interpreting it to be no other than a command from God to open the book, and read the first chapter I should find. For I had heard of Antony, that coming in during the reading of the Gospel, he received the admonition, as if what was being read was spoken to him: Go, sell all that thou hast, and give to the poor, and you shall have treasure in heaven, and come and follow me: and by such oracle he was forthwith converted unto Thee.

Eagerly then I returned to the place where (my friend) Alypius was sitting; for there had I laid the volume of the Apostle when I arose thence. I seized, opened, and in silence read that section on which my eyes first fell: Not in rioting and drunkenness, not in chambering and wantonness, not in strife and envying; but put ye on the Lord Jesus Christ, and make not provision for the flesh, in concupiscence. No further would I read; nor needed I: for instantly at the end of this sentence, by a light as it were of serenity infused into my heart, all the darkness of doubt vanished away.

Tuesday (Fifth Week of Lent)

GOSPEL: JN 8:21–30

Jesus said to the Pharisees: "I am going away and you will look for me, but you will die in your sin. Where I am going you cannot come." So the Jews said, "He is not going to kill himself, is he, because he said, 'Where I am going you cannot come'?" He said to them, "You belong to what is below, I belong to what is above. You belong to this world, but I do not belong to this world. That is why I told you that you will die in your sins. For if you do not believe that I AM, you will die in your sins." So they said to him, "Who are you?" Jesus said to them, "What I told you from the beginning. I have much to say about you in condemnation. But the one who sent me is true, and what I heard from him I tell the world." They did not realize that he was speaking to them of the Father. So Jesus said to them, "When you lift up the Son of Man, then you will realize that I AM, and that I do nothing on my own, but I say only what the Father taught me. The one who sent me is with me. He has not left me alone, because I always do what is pleasing to him." Because he spoke this way, many came to believe in him.

(1) *The new eyes of Christ*

Christ brought a new life to Lazarus and to the adulterous woman. What is the meaning of this new life? Today's readings offer us a first element to understand this. When Jesus enters in our life, we receive new eyes: a new way of looking at the world. We can think about Lazarus after his resurrection and the way he enjoyed his first sunrise after his resurrection. We can also think about love; when we fall in love, everything receives a new light because everything seems to be connected and illuminated by our beloved.

To encounter Christ means to encounter a new light. This experience is what happened to the Magi. They saw a star and its light brought them to the King, baby Jesus. Often we have considered faith as a lack of vision. We speak about faith as blind emotion, a leap in the dark. The artists represent Faith as a beautiful woman with a band covering her eyes. But when Jesus calls us, he does not say: "If you believe, then, close your eyes and follow me." Rather he invites: "Come and see."

In his first encyclical, Pope Francis has reminded us that faith is a light that gives us new eyes to look at the world. Faith is born of an encounter with Jesus who reveals his love. Transformed by this love, we gain fresh vision, new eyes to see (*Lumen fidei*, 3–4). His light is capable of illuminating every aspect of human existence: my studies and my hobbies, my engagement and my marriage, my fatherhood and "grandfather-hood," my sufferings and my joys…

(2) *Healing comes through your eyes: look at the Pierced One*

We are getting closer to the Passion of Jesus. In today's Gospel we see again how the Pharisees do not believe in him. They are not able to recognize him as the Son of God. Even though they have seen so many miracles of Jesus, their eyes are blind. Something similar happens in the first reading (Nm 21). The people of Israel have been saved by God from slavery. They have seen the plagues and the Red Sea opened before them. But now their patience wears out by the journey and they complain against God: "Why have you brought us up from Egypt to die in the wilderness, where there is no food or water?" (Nm 21:5).

We know what happens next. In punishment, the Lord sends among the people seraphim serpents and later the Lord tells Moses to make a bronze serpent and mount it on a pole. And "whenever the serpent bit someone, the person looked at the bronze serpent and recovered" (Nm 21:9). Through their eyes, they are healed and saved.

What is the meaning of this bronze serpent? This serpent is, of course, the sign of God's forgiveness. After Moses' intercession, the

Lord asks him to make it. But can we discover something more here? One night, speaking with Nicodemus, Jesus explains to him (and us) the deeper sense of this event. This serpent was a sign for the future, a sign to be accomplished in Christ. "Just as Moses lifted up the serpent in the desert, so must the Son of Man be lifted up, so that everyone who believes in him may have eternal life" (Jn 3:14–15). What Moses did in the desert will be accomplished in the Passion of Christ at Golgotha. As we read today: "When you lift up the Son of Man, then you will realize that I AM" (Jn 8:28).

Healing comes through our eyes. Like the Israelites in the desert, so us today, looking at Christ. Salvation comes through our contemplation. We become what we contemplate, what we consider in our heart. The little child will become like the heroes he watches in the movies or books he reads. If we look at Christ, we become like him. "They will look upon him whom they have pierced" (Jn 19:37; see Zec 12:10).

As a "new Moses," Jesus lifts up this sign of salvation: a cross instead of a bronze serpent. But there is a great difference. Moses took some bronze and made a serpent, whereas Jesus offers himself, his own body and blood on the Cross. Looking at his greatest love, our eyes are healed.

(3) *Look at me, look at the Father*

What happens in us when we look at Jesus on the Cross? We know very well how to "speak" with our eyes. Looking at someone we communicate so many things. Our sight is not just passive or receptive. With our eyes we are active; we can offend the other, we can give him new hope and trust, we can forgive and express so many things.

Our eyes also reveal to us where our heart is. Richard of Saint Victor, a great medieval theologian said: "Ubi amor, ibi oculus." Where there is love, there is the eye. Tell me where your eye is and I will tell you where your heart is. Love wants to see!

In this way, our contemplation of Jesus helps us to place our heart in the Father. Looking at the Cross we enter into the great movement of love between Jesus and his Father. Through our eyes we belong to him. We can understand in this way the hard words of Jesus: "You belong to what is below, I belong to what is above," that is, to the Father. The Pharisees do not belong to the Father because they are not able to contemplate Jesus.

When we look at the Cross, we are called to grow in our desire of being with him. Jesus wants us to look at him because he wants to reveal to us the great love of the Father. For that reason he has been lifted up. Like the lighthouse which is placed on high to give light to the ships during the night, Jesus is lifted up in the night. His light comes from the past and arrives to us through so many witnesses. And this light comes also from the future, from the Resurrection, opening before us a great path. His light reveals to us how immense is the Father's love.

"Where there is love, there is the eye." What is the food for your eyes? What are the images that fill your eyes and therefore your heart? How often do you look at your spouse with tenderness and forgiveness? How do you keep the presence of your beloved during your workday?

For your prayer

Pray to Mary with the words of Pope Francis (*Lumen fidei*, 60):

Mother, help our faith! Teach us to see all things with the eyes of Jesus, that he may be light for our path. And may this light of faith always increase in us, until the dawn of that undying day which is Christ himself, your Son, our Lord!

Wednesday (Fifth Week of Lent)

GOSPEL: JN 8:31–42

Jesus then said to those Jews who believed in him, "If you remain in my word, you will truly be my disciples, and you will know the truth, and the truth will set you free." They answered him, "We are descendants of Abraham and have never been enslaved to anyone. How can you say, 'You will become free'?" Jesus answered them, "Amen, amen, I say to you, everyone who commits sin is a slave of sin. A slave does not remain in a household forever, but a son always remains. So if the Son frees you, then you will truly be free. I know that you are descendants of Abraham. But you are trying to kill me, because my word has no room among you. I tell you what I have seen in the Father's presence; then do what you have heard from the Father."

They answered and said to him, "Our father is Abraham." Jesus said to them, "If you were Abraham's children, you would be doing the works of Abraham. But now you are trying to kill me, a man who has told you the truth that I heard from God; Abraham did not do this. You are doing the works of your father!" So they said to him, "We are not illegitimate. We have one Father, God." Jesus said to them, "If God were your Father, you would love me, for I came from God and am here; I did not come on my own, but he sent me."

(1) *The new ears of Christ*

We all know people—our father or grandfather, perhaps—who are hard of hearing. We know how it is difficult to speak with them. Great patience is necessary on both sides. When we are hard of hearing we suffer a kind of isolation from the world. We can see, touch, smell, and taste, but everything seems to be mute. Our hardness of hearing tends to isolate us from the others; we don't understand what they say and they have to repeat several times the same comment until they get tired. As long as he is alive Jesus tries to dialogue with those who believe in him and with the Pharisees and scribes.

Today Jesus invites us to follow him: "If you remain in my word, you will truly be my disciples." A disciple is "the one who hears" from his master, the one who remains in his word. To become a disciple requires that we open our ear to Jesus' word. "Morning after morning / he wakens my ear to hear as disciples do; / The Lord GOD opened my ear; / I did not refuse, / did not turn away" (Is 50:4–5).

The new life of Lazarus after his resurrection, our new life after our baptism, implies not only new eyes to see but also new ears to hear. Our hearing is a very humble sense. Sight is powerful and controls everything. But to hear implies to wait; I cannot hear if there is not a word coming to me from outside. For this reason, we do not like to hear. We prefer to speak, to see, to touch, and to transform everything with our hands.

In today's Gospel, Jesus invites us to remain in his word. "My sheep hear my voice; I know them, and they follow me" (Jn 10:27). In this way we are able to know the truth and the truth will set us free (see Jn 8:32–34). What is this truth and this freedom?

When Jesus gives us these difficult words the best thing we can do is look to him, at his own life. Jesus is always remaining in the words of his Father. From its very beginning his life consists in doing the will of the Father. When he comes into the world he says: "Behold, I come to do your will, O God" (Heb 10:7). Jesus is the Son, the one who hears the word of the Father, that is, the one who is obedient. To be obedient (from latin: ob-audire, hearing) means to hear well; this submission is the virtue of the ear. Jesus was never "hard of hearing" to the Father. In his "hour," in Gethsemane, he is obedient until death, and death on a cross. He remains in the word of the Father and he is free.

(2) *Healing through our ears*

This obedience is not the way we usually think about freedom. To be free is not to obey, but rather to do whatever I want. The slave and the child are obedient because they have to. Later, freedom comes when I do not depend on others and I can do my will. We usually think that the ideal person—perfect freedom—is the "self-made" and self-sufficient man; freedom sets us free. But Jesus says today that true freedom comes to us when we become disciples. How is that possible?

Modernity has offered us a sick freedom. We think we are free because we do not depend on others, because we do not need them. Finally this freedom brings us to a complete isolation. The self-made man is alone, is very vulnerable since he has no relationships with others. Nobody can help him because he pretends to be self-sufficient. But this concept of freedom is a crazy idea. We may think of our family life. Sometimes we try to avoid asking for help or for counsel because we think we can resist alone and this destroys us.

True freedom does not come through isolation but through hearing. Our freedom is always an answer to God's call to existence. To be free implies to accept the gift of life, to accept that I depend on others, I need others. And I rejoice in this dependence.

What then is the solution? Slaves or self-made men? Jesus offers us the authentic path: sonship. "Unless you turn and become like children, you will not enter the kingdom of heaven" (Mt 18:3). Acknowledge that you are a child, a son or daughter, and rejoice in this dependence on your Father! Rejoice because even if a mother forget her infant, God will never forget you (see Is 49:15).

True freedom begins through our ears. I accept that I do not have the first word. God is the giver of life; he is the beginning. Human freedom is always an answer to this gift. Through our obedience we become free; we become disciples. It is not the obedience of the slave but a very different one; like Jesus, the Son, we are called to be obedient. Open your ears. Become his disciple, the disciple of his heart!

Following the path of Christ, we find the lives of so many saints that, out of love, were obedient until death. Today's first reading offers us an example of this. Three young men disobeyed the royal command of King Nebuchadnezzar. They yielded their bodies rather than worship any god except the God of Israel. The king cast them into the fire, into the furnace. After some time, the king hears voices from the furnaces. The three young men, saved by God's angel, are singing and praising God. This freedom is also the experience of Peter and the apostles. The Sanhedrin orders them to stop teaching in the name of Jesus, but they reply: "We must obey God rather than men" (Acts 5:29).

(3) *Mary's obedience*

If we are a little hard of hearing we are invited to come closer to Mary, the Mother of God. Before we begin Holy Week she can help us to prepare our heart. Mary is blessed because she believed. Her ears and her heart received the word of God: "Be done to me according to your will!" Saint Ireneaus, a great Father of the Church, helps us to understand the mystery of her obedience. "The knot of Eve's disobedience was untied by the obedience of Mary; what the virgin Eve bound by her unbelief, the Virgin Mary loosened by her faith" (*Adversus Haereses*, III, 22, 4).

Mary unties the knot of sin. Her "yes" opens the door for God to undo the knot of the ancient disobedience. She helps us to loosen the most tangled knots in our life. Sometimes it seems that our life is a huge knot nobody can loosen. Our family life, the struggles in our marriage, the problems with our children, or at work...who can untie this terrible knot? Who can give order to this mess, this chaos? Then we try to untie the knots by just pushing and it is even worse.

> Sin is a terrible knot which seems impossible to untie. When we disobey our parents, a little knot of disobedience is created. When we do not listen to our spouse or we judge him, a little knot is created deep within us. Many knots can form a tangle which gets more and more

> painful and difficult to undo. (Pope Francis, Marian Day during the Year of Faith, October 12, 2013)

Mary is the Mother who patiently brings us to God so that he can untangle the disorder of our relationships. With her help all the knots of our heart can be undone. Ask Mary to help you: "Give me your ears so that I can hear God and answer with my free obedience. Give me your ears so that I can hear my beloved without judgments and prejudices." With Mary we can hear the others in the way Saint Ignatius explains in his Spiritual Exercises:

> Let it be presupposed that every good Christian is to be more ready to save what the neighbor says than to condemn it. If he cannot save it, let him inquire how he means it; and if he means it badly, let him correct him with charity. (*Presupposition*, 22)

With Mary, this attitude is possible!

For your prayer

Pray to Mary with the words of Pope Francis (*Lumen fidei*, 60):

Mother, help our faith! Open our ears to hear God's word and to recognize his voice and call. Awaken in us a desire to follow in his footsteps, to go forth from our own land and to receive his promise. Help us to be touched by his love, that we may touch him in faith. Help us to entrust ourselves fully to him and to believe in his love, especially at times of trial, beneath the shadow of the cross, when our faith is called to mature. Sow in our faith the joy of the Risen One.

Thursday (Fifth Week of Lent)

GOSPEL: JN 8:51–59

Jesus said to the Jews: "Amen, amen, I say to you, whoever keeps my word will never see death." So the Jews said to him, "Now we are sure that you are possessed. Abraham died, as did the prophets, yet you say, 'Whoever keeps my word will never taste death.' Are you greater than our father Abraham, who died? Or the prophets, who died? Who do you make yourself out to be?" Jesus answered, "If I glorify myself, my glory is worth nothing; but it is my Father who glorifies me, of whom you say, 'He is our God.' You do not know him, but I know him. And if I should say that I do not know him, I would be like you a liar. But I do know him and I keep his word. Abraham your father rejoiced to see my day; he saw it and was glad." So the Jews said to him, "You are not yet fifty years old and you have seen Abraham?" Jesus said to them, "Amen, amen, I say to you, before Abraham came to be, I AM." So they picked up stones to throw at him; but Jesus hid and went out of the temple area.

(1) *It is not his hour*

Times are getting worse. We are close to Holy Week and the hatred against Jesus is growing exponentially. A few days ago the Pharisees wanted to stone the adulterous woman together with him. Now, in today's Gospel they want to stone Jesus. The reason is the great promise proclaimed by him; he promises eternal life for those who keep his words. And this assurance implies a great pretension. Only God can promise eternal life. Therefore the Jews try to kill him and they even pick up stones to throw at him.

But his hour is not yet come. Let us remember again that the Passion of Christ will not be an accident, something unexpected. All this suffering will happen as the sign of God's greatest love for humanity. Jesus is prepared to give the gift of himself. He does not want to die, of course, but he is prepared to witness to the immense love of God the

Father and he knows this witness implies rejection and death on the cross. In any case, he comes because he loves the Father and he wants to give us eternal life.

We can imagine in these days right before his Passion, Jesus is praying and meditating on the prophet Isaiah:

> The Lord GOD opened my ear; / I did not refuse, / did not turn away. / I gave my back to those who beat me, / my cheeks to those who tore out my beard; / My face I did not hide from insults and spitting. (Is 50:5–6)

Jesus does not refuse, does not turn away. Not yet, but soon. His hour is at hand. Do you want to be with him?

(2) *A great promise: eternal life*

We hear great promises when elections are close. Sometimes in their speeches the candidates try to gain our votes through promises. They make promises in order to get elected as president, senator... Today Jesus makes the great promise of eternal life. As the fruit of this speech he is not elected or rewarded but he is persecuted and almost stoned.

So great a promise needs great witnesses. During this lent we have seen Jesus together with Moses and Elijah on Mount Tabor. Today Jesus speaks about Abraham, the very beginning and father of the people of Israel. "Before Abraham came to be, I AM!" To promise eternal life implies to offer himself as the true God. The Jews are called to choose; Jesus is really God or he is crazy. Some things can only be done by God. We can remember the question of the Jews when Jesus forgave the sins of the paralytic before healing him: "He is blaspheming. Who but God alone can forgive sins?" (Mk 2:7). Who but God alone can promise eternal life?

Our life, our days are like grass. We blossom like a flower in the field. "A wind sweeps over it and it is gone" (Psalm 103:16). Who can promise us one day more of life? Today Jesus promises eternal life: "Whoever keeps my word will never taste death." Life forever! When she was seven years old, Saint Theresa of Avila really enjoyed reading lives of saints. She would remain amazed thinking about the eternity they were conquering: They rejoice with God forever, forever, forever...!

God makes great promises. He promised an old man called Abram that he would be father of generations. Sarah laughed when she heard that she, already aged, would conceive a child. God makes great promises. Saint Augustine was surprised by this peculiarity of God.

God, who is faithful, put himself in our debt, not by receiving anything but by promising so much. A promise was not sufficient for him; he chose to commit himself in writing as well, as it were making a contract of his promises (Saint Augustine, On the Psalms 109, 1).

God is in our debt. Remember today the promises of God in your life. From your baptism he has promised to take care of you as a Father. From your confirmation day he has promised to give you the strength of the Holy Spirit. From your wedding day he has promised to be with you and your spouse in the joys and sufferings of the journey...

(3) *Fruitfulness forever!*

God makes great promises and accomplishes them. "Whoever keeps my word will never see death" (Jn 8:51). The promise of eternal life causes a great scandal among the Jews. Abraham, the father of the people died, as did the prophets. Jesus comes today remembering that even if Abraham died, the promise of God does not die. Christ tells us that Abraham rejoiced to see his day, the day of Jesus! How is this possible?

Abraham rejoiced when he received the promise of becoming a father. Then a few months later he rejoiced when he saw Sarah's pregnancy and even more later when he embraced Isaac, his son. Now when Jesus has come into the world, Abraham rejoices because he sees that the promise he received several hundred years ago has been accomplished in Jesus.

But Jesus says even more. Not only Abraham sees it now and rejoices, but Jesus says that "Abraham saw it and was glad." When Abraham saw his son Isaac, he realized God was powerful and faithful and he discovered also that the promises of God remain forever. Isaac was the son of the promise but this was not the end of God's words. After Isaac's birth, God continued to promise Abraham greater things: Isaac, Jacob, Joseph... Moses... At the end of this path, as the fulfillment of the promise, God sends the promised one, his Son Jesus Christ. The promises of God are a chain of increasing love and generosity.

God makes great promises and accomplishes them. Sometimes it may seem that he is delaying his answer. But do not be afraid: "The gifts and the call of God are irrevocable" (Rom 11:29).

For your prayer

Remember the promises of the Lord in your life. "I will be with you always." He has not promised there will be no sufferings or problems. He has promised his presence with you forever and the fruitfulness of your life.

Friday (Fifth Week of Lent)

GOSPEL: JN 10:31–42

The Jews again picked up rocks to stone him. Jesus answered them, "I have shown you many good works from my Father. For which of these are you trying to stone me?" The Jews answered him, "We are not stoning you for a good work but for blasphemy. You, a man, are making yourself God." Jesus answered them, "Is it not written in your law, 'I said, "You are gods"'? If it calls them gods to whom the word of God came, and scripture cannot be set aside, can you say that the one whom the Father has consecrated and sent into the world blasphemes because I said, 'I am the Son of God'? If I do not perform my Father's works, do not believe me; but if I perform them, even if you do not believe me, believe the works, so that you may realize and understand that the Father is in me and I am in the Father." Then they tried again to arrest him; but he escaped from their power.

He went back across the Jordan to the place where John first baptized, and there he remained. Many came to him and said, "John performed no sign, but everything John said about this man was true." And many there began to believe in him.

(1) *The new life of Christ: divinization*

We began our time of Lent with ashes and considering the great desires of Saint Francis Xavier. At the end of this fifth week, Jesus shows us the foundations of this greatness in our heart. The new life brought to Lazarus belongs to the divine plan: Jesus wants us to become his friends.

In today's Gospel we do not need any word of Jesus; from the very beginning, the Jews are already prepared with stones. Whatever he says or does, they have already decided what to do. Of course, if we go to the previous verses of the Gospel we see what has made the Jews angry with Jesus again: "The Father and I are one." They want to stone him for blasphemy: "You, a man, are making yourself God" (Jn 10:32).

In his answer Jesus, as usual, surprises us. He changes our point of view: "Why are you upset because I say that I am one with the Father? Just read the Scripture that says: You are gods, offspring of the Most High (see Ps 82:6). You are angry because I make myself God, but this is nothing special. You think I try to be very high, but this is because you are very low. It is not that I pretend too much but that you have reduced your desires."

Jesus takes advantage of the accusation of blasphemy to reveal our high vocation. We are not called to be obedient slaves of God but his children, his intimate friends. As the Greek Father of the Church, Saint Athanasius put it, our vocation is our "divinization." Through the action of the Holy Spirit we become like God, without losing our humanity.

It is time to remember the beauty of our vocation. "The Son of God became man so that we might become God" (Saint Athanasius, *On the Incarnation*, 54, 3). Our divinization is the goal of the whole project of God, of the creation of the world and his Incarnation. God is not our enemy; he desires our happiness. He wants us to be his friends.

Finally Jesus will close the discussion with an a fortiori argument: "And if this is true, if you are called to be like God, much more I, the Son of God, am God eternally, before all ages. The Father is in me and I am in the Father. Why do you want to kill me?"

(2) *Mediocrity against our high vocation*

The answer of Jesus helps us to understand the essence and root of sin. We usually think that sin—pride, envy, greed, etc.—comes because we try to have things that are greater than us, things that are higher. And in a sense, this is true: we look for the best place during dinner, we try to have the last word in our dialogue at home... But according to Jesus' words, we can better describe our sin as a lack of really great desires. The real face of sin is mediocrity and despair; sin reduces our heart, our desires, our expectations. "Great expectations" is not only a novel of Charles Dickens but also a nice description of our Christian life. Great promises and great expectations.

A few years ago, Benedict XVI made this point clear: "One of the greatest evils of our time is...mediocrity in the questions of faith. Let us not deceive ourselves... If we are Catholic, this must be seen in every area of our life" (Address, June 5 2011, quoting Blessed Cardinal Stepinac). Do not lower the bar. You are not called to a comfortable life but to happiness, holiness, and fruitfulness. Do not to be content with second best. Have the courage to "place your deepest hopes in God alone, not in money, in a career, in worldly success, or in our relationships with others, but in God" (Benedict XVI, London, September 17, 2010).

Mediocrity is not human. God has created us. What he wants most of all for each one of us is that we should become holy. He wants the very best for us which is, by far, our holiness. We may see this from very far when we are struggling with the basic elements of our marriage. But this holiness is really our vocation. We are pilgrims, so we are in progress, but we need to remember every day, every morning the beauty of our vocation. We need to repeat again and again the mysterious words of Saint Paul: "Eye has not seen, and ear has not heard, / and what has not entered the human heart, / what God has prepared for those who love him" (1 Cor 2:9). Among those of you reading this book there are—I am sure!—some of the future saints of the twenty-first century: holy spouses, holy students, holy grandparents... We cannot imagine what God has prepared!

(3) *The mysterious path toward divinization*

While we consider these beautiful things, we may forget today is the Friday before Palm Sunday. In some countries like in the Philippines, Latin American countries, and Spain this day is called "Friday of Sorrows." Today we commemorate the sufferings and solitude of the Blessed Virgin Mary in these days, right before the Passion of her son.

The first reading of the prophet Jeremiah (Jer 20) helps us to understand what is going on in these days in the heart of Jesus and Mary.

Like Jeremiah, Mary finds terror on every side, denunciation, and persecution. "All those who were my friends / are on the watch for any misstep of mine" (Jer 20: 10). After these three years following her son, Mary perceives that something is going to happen. She looks at her son, she hears what the people say about him and she fears for him. But in all this Mary knows that her son is the Son of the Father. In the middle of this sorrow she trusts in the Lord. "But the LORD is with me, like a mighty champion: / ... Sing to the LORD, / praise the LORD, / For he has rescued the life of the poor" (Jer 20:11, 13).

Our divinization comes through the Cross of Christ. With Mary we understand that our high vocation to holiness implies our daily family life, our work, our mission of education... Holiness will not come in a second. A high goal implies great patience. As Rilke, the poet used to say, "whatever passes very quickly cannot sanctify."

For your prayer

Next week we will celebrate the death and resurrection of Christ: his victory over sin and death. Prepare yourself for the greatest days of the year with Mary. We can only understand what will happen next week with the help and counsel of Mary: *Ad Jesum per Mariam.* We arrive to Jesus through Mary.

May the Blessed Mother of God, *Causa nostrae laetitiae,* "Cause of our joy," accompany and support us in the effort to free our heart from slavery to sin. Give us great desires, Virgin Mary!

Saturday (Fifth Week of Lent)

GOSPEL: JN 11:45–56

Many of the Jews who had come to Mary and seen what Jesus had done began to believe in him. But some of them went to the Pharisees and told them what Jesus had done. So the chief priests and the Pharisees convened the Sanhedrin and said, "What are we going to do? This man is performing many signs. If we leave him alone, all will believe in him, and the Romans will come and take away both our land and our nation." But one of them, Caiaphas, who was high priest that year, said to them, "You know nothing, nor do you consider that it is better for you that one man should die instead of the people, so that the whole nation may not perish." He did not say this on his own, but since he was high priest for that year, he prophesied that Jesus was going to die for the nation, and not only for the nation, but also to gather into one the dispersed children of God. So from that day on they planned to kill him.

So Jesus no longer walked about in public among the Jews, but he left for the region near the desert, to a town called Ephraim, and there he remained with his disciples.

Now the Passover of the Jews was near, and many went up from the country to Jerusalem before Passover to purify themselves. They looked for Jesus and said to one another as they were in the temple area, "What do you think? That he will not come to the feast?"

(1) *Human projects and calculations*

What do you think? Will he come to the feast? In today's Gospel we do not see Jesus' actions but the discussions and decisions made about him. Jesus is gone and the people are divided. Some of them, after Lazarus' resurrection, begin to believe in him. Others accuse him before the Pharisees. But Jesus does not defend himself; he is gone to Ephraim, near the desert, to stay with his disciples preparing the great week of his witness.

The Pharisees are also preparing the great week. If he comes to Jerusalem, what are we going to do? Caiaphas, the high priest, gives them the solution: "It is better for you that one man should die instead of the people, so that the whole nation may not perish" (see Jn

11). Niccolò Machiavelli, the Italian politician and historian (author of The Prince) would be happy to hear this argument. Fifteen centuries before, Caiaphas follows the counsels of the Italian about what a leader should do. "If you can kill your enemy, do so; otherwise, try to be his friend." The "good prince" knows this "law" very well. We can kill a just person in order to save many. We can do evil in order to obtain something good. Since Jesus is becoming famous and this is dangerous for the nation, it is right to kill him.

We know the irony of the history. Caiaphas proposes to do an injustice in order to save their lives. But about forty years later, the Romans will come and destroy the whole city. Human calculations do not have the last word.

Saint John offers us another point of view regarding history. The beloved disciple writes his Gospel after the resurrection of the Lord and he is able to understand the divine project that is wiser than any human calculations. For that reason, he is able to discover that Caiaphas "did not say this on his own." In Caiaphas' planning, something greater is coming about. As he says, but in a very different sense, Jesus is going to die for the nation "and not only for the nation, but also to gather into one the dispersed children of God." Saint John sees the big picture, the great vision. Human councils have decided Jesus' death and they do not know that all this belongs to a greater project. God, of course, does not want this evil to happen: the Father does not want Caiaphas to decide this injustice, nor Pilate to be a coward... But God is able to transform this decision and include it in the great history of our salvation. John has this big picture: "You know nothing, Caiaphas, but you are right. It is better. He will die for the people so that the whole nation may not perish. Not as you think, but in a deeper and more true way."

We can ask the Lord to understand with John the big picture of my life. There is a divine plan for me. Similar to Caiaphas, you may think your life is just the consequences of different human decisions, right or wrong. But if you look deeper, you will discover the plan of God. It is a new measure of love, overflowing and generous.

At the end of this week, we better understand the new life brought to us by Jesus. Like Lazarus we live a new life that implies a new way of looking at and hearing the others. It is life eternal, the vocation to become like God. In our first reading (Ez 37) we hear about this great gathering. God will rebuild, he will make a new covenant of peace. He is the Lord, the shepherd who gathers us together.

(2) *Keeping in your heart with Mary*

Saint John received these new eyes to understand the world because he stayed with Mary during the Passion of Jesus. John had a great master: the Mother of God. As Origen, a great Father of the Church says, to understand the life of Jesus we need to be like Saint John; we need to repose our head on the heart of Christ, and to stay with Mary at the foot of the Cross. If we really want to understand what is going to happen during Holy Week we need to remain with Mary and to enter into her heart.

What is going on in the heart of Mary? While Caiaphas and the Jews are planning, another Jew, Mary, is keeping everything in her heart, trying to understand the meaning of all these things according to the divine plan (see Lk 2:51). Traveling from Nazareth to Bethlehem, she was keeping in her heart the sense of this difficult trip. Escaping to Egypt, coming back to Nazareth, looking for Jesus, lost and found in the temple...she was considering everything and asking God for his light. Now when Caiaphas is planning the death of her son, Mary may remember the plot of King Herod against the baby Jesus. On that occasion the angel saved them and they escaped. Now the "hour" of Jesus has arrived; it is the time of the great gift of himself. Now the words and promises of the Archangel Gabriel seem to be contradicted but Mary remains, standing firm in faith.

I invite you to take Mary as the companion of your path. You may have so many events in your life that you do not understand yet: crosses, anxieties, misunderstandings... Ask Mary to keep her wisdom in your heart and so discover the hand of God in each event. Perhaps the crosses of your daily life seem to contradict the great promises of your marriage or of your religious vocation. Do not be afraid. Ask Mary to be the companion of your life. Enter into the company of the Savior!

(3) *"I renew everything"*

What do you think? Will he come to the feast? Mary knows he will. For this reason he came into the world, to give witness of the truth, to reveal the great love of God our Father.

Jesus knows that they plan to kill him. What do you think? Is he coming to the feast, that is, to his death and burial? Perhaps he will remain in a safe and comfortable place? Stay with Mary and give me the right answer: Yes! He comes to save us, he comes to proclaim the love of God the Father. "Behold, I come to do your will, O God" (Heb 10:7).

In the movie *The Passion of the Christ* of Mel Gibson, we find a beautiful moment in which Jesus encounters his mother. Carrying the cross he falls and Mary comes to help him: "I am here." Jesus then looks at her and reminds her: "You see, Mother. I renew everything" (see Rev 21:5). Yes. He comes to renew everything. It is not Caiaphas but Jesus who guides the rhythm of the Passion. It is not haphazard or bad luck, but God himself who guides my life.

Tomorrow we begin Holy Week. Ask the Lord: Help me to recognize your presence, the good shepherd in my life. In these days, Jesus wants to renew your heart, your relationships. Through his water of life, he comes to transform your ash into a new creature.

For your prayer

Today I invite you to pray to Mary with the beautiful hymn we find at the end of the daily Liturgy of the Hours: "Loving Mother of the Redeemer" (*Alma Redemptoris Mater*):

Loving Mother of the Redeemer,
gate of heaven, star of the sea,
assist your people who have fallen yet strive to rise again.
To the wonderment of nature you bore your Creator,
yet remained a virgin after as before.
You who received Gabriel's joyful greeting,
have pity on us poor sinners.

SOLEMNITIES DURING LENT

Solemnity of Saint Joseph: March 19th

GOSPEL: MT 1:16, 18–21, 24A

(Note: A different Gospel may be used)

Jacob [was] the father of Joseph, the husband of Mary. Of her was born Jesus who is called the Christ.

Now this is how the birth of Jesus Christ came about. When his mother Mary was betrothed to Joseph, but before they lived together, she was found with child through the Holy Spirit. Joseph her husband, since he was a righteous man, yet unwilling to expose her to shame, decided to divorce her quietly. Such was his intention when, behold, the angel of the Lord appeared to him in a dream and said, "Joseph, son of David, do not be afraid to take Mary your wife into your home. For it is through the Holy Spirit that this child has been conceived in her. She will bear a son and you are to name him Jesus, because he will save his people from their sins." When Joseph awoke, he did as the angel of the Lord had commanded him and took his wife into his home.

(1) *Joseph, the man of trust*

If we want to learn humility, today we receive a wonderful example and master. Saint Joseph's whole life is a path of humility. In one passage of his *Divine Comedy,* Dante tells us of his encounter with his great "heroes." Virgil, his rescuer, guide, and counselor, introduces him to the greatest poets of the ancient times: Homer, Ovid, Lucan, Horace (circle 1, canto 4). During this imaginary encounter Dante seems like a small child among great and wise men, like an ant between elephants.

We can think of Saint Joseph's life in Nazareth in similar terms. He is living among "the greatest saints" of the history of the world, Jesus and Mary. In this way, speaking, praying, resting, and working with them, he becomes a huge saint. The closer you get to high peaks as those in the Rocky Mountains, the higher you go.

I remember having watched a movie about Saint Mary and Saint Joseph. We were the whole community together. According to some good friends we were prepared to watch a wonderful movie about Mary, mother of Jesus and "daughter of her Son" (according to one of the titles given by Dante in the *Divine Comedy*). Actually, we did not finish the movie since it was not worthy. One of the worst moments was the description of Saint Joseph as a sad and even bitter man who was "a father without a child and a spouse without a wife." But this is not Joseph!

Of course, Joseph's marriage is very special since it is virginal, and his fatherhood is an adoptive one because Jesus is the eternal Son of God and the son of Mary in the flesh. But Joseph has a really wonderful mission. He is "father" of Jesus according to the law, insofar he is called to give him the name of "Jesus"! He is husband of Mary and he protects her and has a very special friendship with her.

Here we can discover the great vocation of Joseph and his great humility. Joseph is God's man of trust and it is into his custody that God entrusted his most precious treasures. During Joseph's life, he does not shine, he makes no wonders, but remains "in the shadow."

(2) *Joseph, the best man*

The following comparison may help us to understand better Joseph's humility and vocation. God is preparing the "wedding" of his eternal Son with human nature. He wants to send his Son to the world as one of us. He needs Mary, as the Mother of God and he will receive her "permission" through the message of Saint Gabriel. But he also needs someone to take care of the logistics: finding the way from Nazareth to Bethlehem, moving quickly to Egypt, buying a new house in Nazareth, taking care of the incomes… This man, the best man of the wedding, is Saint Joseph. He prepares the celebration, he pays attention to every detail but he remains unseen, hidden, in the shadow.

Saint Joseph helps us to give without proclaiming our merits. Our left hand must not know what our right hand is doing. This deep humility helps Saint Joseph to do great things. In his life we find together humility and greatness of heart. In fact, he receives missions that are too big for him: "Am I, Joseph, called to live with the Messiah and to take care of him?" His humility makes him understand: "Yes. You will name him Jesus."

Our humility helps us to accept great missions. It is not because of our merits that we receive this task. It is God's action with us. And in our marriage, our work, our charity with our parents, or our mission of education…we have a share in Joseph's vocation. We are also called to bear Jesus in our children, to generate them into life eternal through their baptism and education.

(3) *Joseph the strong*

As the man of trust and the best man, Joseph will accomplish his mission: Redemptoris custos! The guardian of the Redeemer, Jesus Christ! Following Christ, humility and greatness of heart go together. We trust in the Lord, who gives us missions that are bigger than us. We are called to grow together with our vocation.

The mission of Joseph is also our mission. As fathers, mothers, priests…we receive the great gift of the presence of the Redeemer: our marriage, our children, our spiritual fatherhood, our mission of study and work, our brothers and sisters at our parish, our neighbors… We are called to be *Redemptoris custos*, that is, guardians of the Redeemer!

In the beginning of the bible, we see a person who is very different. Out of jealousy, Cain killed his brother Abel. Then God asked him: "'Where is your brother Abel?' He answered, 'I do not know. Am I my brother's keeper?'" (Gn 4:9). Joseph knows very well he is the keeper, the protector, and guardian of God's most precious gift: Jesus and Mary. He takes care of them, and thanks to him, we receive Jesus as our Savior and Mary as our Mother. Thank you, Joseph!

I am my "brother's keeper"! Who do I look at in my marriage, my family, the people I encounter every day? Do I realize the Lord wants me and needs me to take care of them, as Saint Joseph did with Jesus and Mary? We need the strength of Saint Joseph to be faithful to our mission!

For your prayer

Today stay with Saint Joseph in prayer. You can pray with him the Magnificat.

"Most beloved father, dispel the evil and falsehood and sin…graciously assist us from heaven in our struggle with the powers of darkness…and just as once you saved the Child Jesus from mortal danger, so now defend God's holy Church from the snares of her enemies and from all adversity" (John Paul II, *Redemptoris custos,* 31).

Solemnity of the Annunciation of the Lord: March 25th

GOSPEL: LK 1:26–38

The angel Gabriel was sent from God to a town of Galilee called Nazareth, to a virgin betrothed to a man named Joseph, of the house of David, and the virgin's name was Mary. And coming to her, he said, "Hail, full of grace! The Lord is with you." But she was greatly troubled at what was said and pondered what sort of greeting this might be. Then the angel said to her, "Do not be afraid, Mary, for you have found favor with God. Behold, you will conceive in your womb and bear a son, and you shall name him Jesus. He will be great and will be called Son of the Most High, and the Lord God will give him the throne of David his father, and he will rule over the house of Jacob forever, and of his Kingdom there will be no end." But Mary said to the angel, "How can this be, since I have no relations with a man?" And the angel said to her in reply, "The Holy Spirit will come upon you, and the power of the Most High will overshadow you. Therefore the child to be born will be called holy, the Son of God. And behold, Elizabeth, your relative, has also conceived a son in her old age, and this is the sixth month for her who was called barren; for nothing will be impossible for God." Mary said, "Behold, I am the handmaid of the Lord. May it be done to me according to your word." Then the angel departed from her.

(1) *Rejoice, full of grace!*

Exactly nine months before Christmas, on March 25th, we celebrate the solemnity of the Annunciation of the Lord. Liturgical pregnancies are quite exact. Today we do not stop our path toward Easter, but we receive a great light for it. If yesterday Nazareth was the closed place, today we find there a virgin who is completely open to God's plan.

Mary receives the great news from Gabriel. "You will conceive a son and he will be called the Son of the Most High." Through the archangel, God explains his desire to Mary. She has been chosen to be the Mother of the Messiah, the mother of God. The earth is not called to be a desert because the Creator of heaven and earth, the stream of living water, is coming to Mary and through her, to all humanity. Let us rejoice!

(2) *How can this be?*

We can consider now Mary's question. Mary is completely obedient to the Lord and she knows she is called to virginity. What is the meaning of this message? For that reason she asks the angel: "How can this be?" You will not find in her heart any doubt or mistrust, but the desire for understanding the words of God. Zechariah received a similar announcement, asked, and was punished because he did not believe. Mary asks because she wants to obey with her whole heart; she wants to understand the wisdom and beauty of God's plan.

Do not be afraid. God does not want to have slaves, but sons and daughters. He wants us to be like Mary, rejoicing in our obedience. We are not called to obey just as servants, but with joy and understanding. Of course, sometimes we will have to say: "Lord, I do not understand and I do not enjoy doing this, but I trust in you." But our goal, the perfect obedience of the children of God, is full of joy and of increasing understanding. "Do whatever he tells us." And we try to do it with joy, understanding, and "to the brim."

(3) *Behold, I am the handmaid of the Lord*

The dialogue between Mary and the Archangel finishes with the great and unconditional "Yes" to God's plan. Heaven, earth, and God himself were waiting for what Mary would say. Her answer is the door through which God is able to enter the world, to become man. Mary receives today the gift of being Mother of God. She becomes a great river of living water. Through her generous "Yes" to God, the world is transfigured and her heart is transformed by the action of God. Mary receives a gift greater than whatever she could ever imagine. This encounter is the way of God; his gifts are always greater. We are never able to overcome him in generosity.

The saints have followed the example of Mary's complete obedience in their lives. Saint Maria Maravillas of Jesus was canonized in Madrid (Spain) by Pope John Paul II in 2003. She died in December 1974, while repeating: "what a joy to die a Carmelite." During her life she established many Carmels, as a new Saint Theresa of Jesus. During the many trials she endured she used to repeat: "What God wants. When God wants. How God wants."

For your prayer

Pray with the words of Mary, the words of the Angelus. Perhaps you want to remember the dialogue between Jesus and the Samaritan woman and compare it with this one between the Archangel Gabriel and the Nazarene woman.

Made in the USA
Middletown, DE
02 March 2025

71962805R00134